Soccer Training for Goalkeepers
Training Sessions for All Age Groups

SOCCER TRAINING FOR GOALKEEPERS

BISCHOPS/GERARDS/WALLRAFF

TRAINING SESSIONS FOR ALL AGE GROUPS

MEYER
& MEYER
SPORT

Original Title: Fußballtorwart – Das neue Training
© 2000 by Meyer & Meyer Verlag, Aachen

British Library Cataloguing in Publication Data
A catalogue record for this book is available from the British Library

Soccer Training for Goalkeepers
Training Sessions for all Age Groups
Oxford: Meyer & Meyer Sport (UK) Ltd., 2006
ISBN 10: 1-84126-186-6
ISBN 13: 978-1-84126-186-7

© 2006 by Meyer & Meyer Sport (UK) Ltd.
Aachen, Adelaide, Auckland, Budapest, Graz, Johannesburg,
New York, Olten (CH), Oxford, Singapore, Toronto
Member of the World
Sports Publishers' Association (WSPA)
www.w-s-p-a.org
Printed and bound by: B.O.S.S Druck und Medien GmbH, Germany
ISBN 10: 1-84126-186-6
ISBN 13: 978-1-84126-186-7
E-Mail: verlag@m-m-sports.com
www.m-m-sports.com

CONTENTS

FOREWORD
THE GOALKEEPER

Wherever you are, the goalkeeper is held as the madman who stands in the goal because he is too lazy to run about, and moreover because he isn't good enough to play soccer in other positions.

This viewpoint has been totally superceded, particularly by experts, and nobody should shy away, even as a youngster, from standing as goalkeeper because of this. In recent years, particularly, the value of the "last man out" has risen also internationally. For sure, it was the change in the rules by FIFA, where the goalkeeper may no longer touch the ball with the hands following a back-pass, that brought this about. Nowadays, the goalkeeper must also possess good soccer skills. The most fitting term for him would now be 'the all-rounder'.

Jens Lehmann,
Arsenal London

This change in the esteem of the goalkeeper should be enough incentive for young 'soccerites' to choose to be the one who always is taking up the 'rear'. Contrary to a lot of prejudice, there is no other position on the field than the Number 1 who has to train so intensively. Simply from the fact that the ball may be allowed to be played by all parts of the body within the home penalty area means, besides having good coordination and movement technical skills, the body must be well built and muscular (after puberty) in order to physically withstand the inevitable hard shots that are made at goal.

One of the most important characteristics of a goalkeeper is often never taken into consideration. He is the chief organizer of the way that the team arranges and plays the defense, so that the other team doesn't get a chance to shoot at goal. The saying "many hands make light work" comes to mind here also for modern soccer today, because practically every goal scored is a decisive one. The Number 1 doesn't perhaps play as spectacularly as the others, but by good "coaching" contributes more success to the team as a whole. Because of this, goalkeepers nowadays are mainly no dullards, but rather are some of the best-qualified and educated members of a team. This comes about because they have to deal with the organization of the team defense, and because they have to be rhetorically in a position to place the defenders correctly.

All these things should be an incentive to have fun in goal as an 'all-rounder' and to be able, every now and again, to shine.

Yours
Jens Lehmann,
Arsenal London

Waiting for the ball

THE GOALKEEPER'S NEW ROLE

"Simply, by virtue of the rules of the game, the goalkeeper has a special position on the field. This is because the goalkeeper's performance is not merely an eleventh of the team's efforts. An outstanding goalkeeper can more or less 'save the day' on his own and thus becomes the backbone of the team. On the other hand, a boob by the Number 1 can also tip the game." This statement by Jörg Daniel, ex German National League Goalkeeper and Football Union Trainer, characterizes the dimensions in which goalkeepers can play themselves into.

Through the change in the rules – the back-pass rule – introduced at the beginning of the 90s, the acrobatic and punching all-rounder not only has to show good reflexes on the goal line and good control of the penalty area, he is also required to demonstrate good soccer ability both in the defensive as well as the offensive.

This development, however, has to have a corresponding successful training regime in that besides the special training for the goalkeeper as the main part of his involvement, he has to become an important part of the team in all its individual elements.

Goalkeeper training, designed for children and youths, however, has to fit the developing circumstances. The content of such training has to, due to the growing up and maturity processes of young people, include the various elements of the game and the intensity and build up of the training. Taking note of the psychological development in these predetermined patterns is therefore an absolute prerequisite.

The goalkeeper in modern soccer plays a double function: As the last defensive player on his side, he has to face all the efforts of the opposing team using all his capabilities. When in possession of the ball, he is the designer and initiator of the attack of his own team. Coming from a player, who has to 'hold' the ball, this active 'soccer player' has to become the game deciding Number 1.

Klaus Bischops,
Heinz-Willi Gerards,
Jürgen Wallraff

Notice where
the hands
are

1 THE NUMBER ONE AND THE UNDERSTANDING OF HIS¹ NEW ROLE

Like all players in a team, the goalkeeper also follows the aim of getting the ball into possession of his team as soon as the 'round piece of leather' is being played amongst the opposition. Contrary to his other players on the team, in the penalty area he can use his hands. However, there are limitations to this since the introduction of the back-pass rule.

A further development within the tactical structure of soccer has lead, despite the change in the rules, to an increase in the number of back-passes to the own goal. In this way, the goalkeeper's work has increased somewhat. He is increasingly brought in as the first offensive player in his team and his passing kick up the field initiates the kind of attack and its quality. In order to capitalize on this success, it requires soccer expertise with the equipment. The goalkeeper, up until now the one who caught and held the ball and was mainly trained as a defensive player, needs to be able to plan tactically with an eye for offensive play and technical ability, in order to put the opportunities recognized into effect.

This expertise to be able to play soccer well, also in defense, is an indispensable factor. Tactical game play, such as the 4 fullbacks defense system, playing the other team offside or stopping a steep, flanking, opposing attack requires that the goalkeeper has to, under certain circumstances, assume a kind of position as the sweeper or "libero", demanding certain playing potential.

Although he has taken on a 'special role' in the team because of his job profile, he has become an important element of his team both in defense and on the attack, thanks to latest tactical thinking. Compared with the 3 or 4 defense systems, soccer has seen for decades now the midfield 3 or 4 system, placed 'longitudinally'. This means that we now have another picture in which the goalkeeper is involved.

Teams that are particularly successful are those that employ a central attack axis – goalkeeper, sweeper, midfield player, spearhead attacker and can play at top level.

---

¹ The male form is used throughout the book for simplicity and easy reading. In all respects the female form is equally valid and included.

On the one hand, this gives an alternative to the much extolled wing attack, and at the same time broadens the tactical palette of the team. On the other hand, the goalkeeper has a distinct function if he is faced with such an axial attack, as being at the 'end of the line' so to speak.

Similarly, he could be the start of such an action with his efforts to start an attack. His ability to spot situations rapidly and open up accurate passing through this axis can open up decisive, game chances for his team. On this Ottmar Hitzfeld states, "In every top team, there is a central axis, which leads the team. This axis is the factor that radiates the personality and the identity of such a team." And a good keeper simply is all part of this and can lead the game from the rear.

This is why the improvement of understanding game play and soccer skills must consequentially be also included in daily routine training alongside the inevitable individual training. The requirement is to carry out goalkeeper training in a game form together with the team or parts of the team, so that the goalkeeper is confronted with typical, competitive situations. The field players can be given tasks to vary the exercises.

CONCLUSIONS/SUMMARY

- The goalkeeper must receive individual schooling in skills for keeping the goal.
- He needs to have soccer skills in his role as 'vice-sweeper' and 'attack initiator' for his team, and these skills can be acquired by participating in team training.
- As the 'main stay' of his team he must practice competitive situations with the whole team or with part groups so that they can get as near as possible to realistic play in training.

In play, goalkeepers are no cavaliers.
They always have to have priority on the ball!

2 WHAT MUST A GOALKEEPER BE ABLE TO DO AND HOW SHOULD HE TRAIN?

Since the content of training sessions for all age groups stem from the demands of the competitive game, the performance factors for effective and game situational training for the goalkeeper can be gained by carrying out a critical analysis. Besides fitness and skills ability as a basis for the must-does, tactics and psychological aspects are also important factors. The 'engaged' goalkeeper needs a direct bonding in the team game; in short, he must be capable of 'reading' the game and be able to shape it.

Using keywords, a table with the job profile has been constructed. The abilities required of a good goalkeeper have been divided into five different areas.

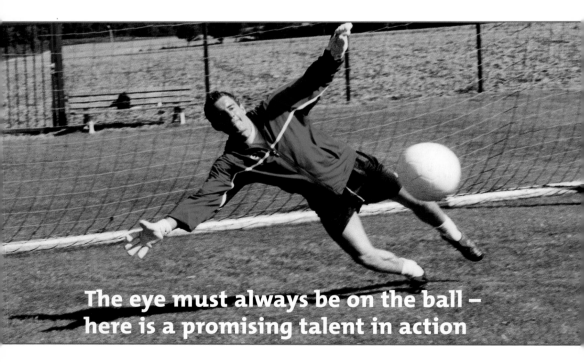

The eye must always be on the ball – here is a promising talent in action

JOB PROFILE – GOALKEEPER

Basic Techniques	Catching the ball, punching the ball away, diving after the ball, jumping, goal kicks, kick outs, controlling the ball with the foot, dribbling, playing around and outplaying the opposition.
Basic Fitness	Flexibility, ability to react, coordination, speed, take-off power.
Basic Tactics	Organizing the defense, positional play, control of the penalty box, standard situations, winning a tackle one on one.
Mental Characteristics – Basics	Concentration, commitment, daring, self-confidence, equanimity, anticipation, coping with stress, (It's well known that games are won in the head!)
Game Creativity – Abilities	Be able to read the intentions of fellow players and the opposition, be able to intervene into the game at the right time and in the right situation, judge the player's direction, be able to develop a sense of game situations.

By looking closer at the goalkeeper's job profile, the importance of German Union Trainer Detlev Brüggemann's observation will be quickly recognized: "The goalkeeper is none other than the most active player of a team nearest to its own goal."

In this function he cannot be differentiated from the remainder of the team. His constant play together with the field players becomes a fundamental basic factor. This aspect of goalkeeping has, of course, consequences for the schooling of goalkeepers at all performance levels and for all age groups. The inclusion of the goalkeeper in complex training exercises with the field players is the order of the day.

Goalkeeper training can only be carried out by playing realistic game exercises!
Detlev Brüggemann

Ex-German League Goalkeeper Jörg Daniel justifiably points out a problem correctly regarding training. Lots of trainers know very little about goalkeeping techniques and tactics from their own sports experience. This lack of knowledge leads to the fact that the right basic situations of goalkeeping in training are not made transparent by movement sequences and as a result, the necessary tactical tips are not forthcoming.

Therefore, goalkeeper training should be combined as often as possible with team training. On the other hand, individual training should not only be carried out by the instructor, co-instructor, reserve goalkeeper or a defense player, but also every now and again with offensive players so that reality is brought in using 'genuine' attacking players and he has to get used to them.

And finally, the goalkeeper can take part as a field player where the role as an attacker will be interesting for him, because he can experience the reactions of his colleagues.

TYPE OF TRAINING FOR THE GOALKEEPER

	Individual Training	Team/Group Training
Fitness	xx	xx
Technique	xx	xxx
Tactics	x	xxx
Mental Aspects	xx	xx
Game Creativity	x	xxx

xxx = mainly necessary/ xx = necessary/ x = limited

"The goalkeeper must have good soccer skills and be able to kick with either foot"
Erich Ribbeck, former German National Coach

Summarizing, we can observe that the training regime of the goalkeeper should be organized as varied as possible, so that he can operate well in front of his own goal, often as the last player. Therefore, goalkeeping training must be built directly into team training. The goalkeeper must train as often as possible with the team to develop his playing skills and to become integrated into the game play his team employs. Because individual training still has its value in view of the new aim, he has to stand back from some of the team and from competitive training in order to do this.

There is also the task of organizing the individual learning aspects to match the appropriate age and development phases, where children and youths are concerned. Only a long-term, structured training of youths will fit the budding goalkeeper to pick up his necessary skills.

A good goalkeeper reads the body language of
the opposition and their intentions!

3 GOALKEEPING – BASIC TECHNIQUES

As already determined, the role of the goalkeeper and the necessary basic techniques should be learned from childhood by playing, because every keeper should 'grow' into this task.

This state of affairs, but also the fact, that goalkeepers are particularly "types on their own" and are best off learning in their own way, means that a laid down, methodical method that is too strict and differentiating, is not the right approach.

Practical experience from the game and training and the knowledge of his own strengths and weaknesses allow him, in time, to develop **his own** style. Of course one of the tasks of the training instructor is to correct mistakes and give advice from his own observations.

Subsequently, the individual techniques are introduced and the main criteria and possible mistakes that could develop are discussed. However, a detailed, methodical step by step approach is done away with, as every goalkeeper wishes to work up his own profile in training.

It is clear, however, that in goalkeeping training, both the components of "technique" in individual training and "application" of those techniques, combined with positional play and tactics must be covered adequately in team play.

While one can start individual training with an "ideal" technique, sometimes this cannot be put into practice perfectly, or its execution is only possible in a limited way.

For the description of the specific goalkeeping techniques, it is again the game situations that form the starting point for their nomenclature.

WHAT MUST THE GOALKEEPER REACT TO?

Defensive
- Low shots
- Mid-height shots
- High shots
- Low shots into the goal corner
- Mid-height shots into the goal corner
- Shots at point blank range
- Shots near the body
- Flanking passes from the side
- 1 on 1 situations
- Lob shots over the goalkeeper
- Standard situations
  (corners, free kicks, penalties)

Offensive
- Control of the ball with the foot
- Control of the ball with the hand
- Receiving passes from own players
- Control of headers from own players

How can the goalkeeper react?

Goalkeeper techniques can be divided into two areas:
- Techniques for blocking the ball (defensive).
- Techniques for opening own team's play (offensive).

POSITIONAL PLAY

Defensive – Blocking		Offensive – Build up of Play
1 Catching		A Goal kick
2 Collecting (the ball)		B Kick out
3 Punching	On Guard Position	C Throw out
4 Diving (after the ball)		D Rolling pass
5 Foot defense		E Passing
6 Deflecting (the ball)		

On guard position

On guard position

Criteria
- ⚽ Place legs shoulder-width apart.
- ⚽ Knees slightly bent.
- ⚽ Body weight placed over the balls of the feet.
- ⚽ Arms stretched out forming an angle.
- ⚽ Body tensed.
- ⚽ Eye on the ball or the game situation.

Mistakes
- ⚽ Legs / Position of feet too close together – leads to imbalance.
- ⚽ Feet too wide apart – creates a tunnel.
- ⚽ Upper body too upright or knees bent too far – longer reaction time needed.
- ⚽ Body weight centered over the heels.

Bring both hands behind the ball

1) Catching the ball

Criteria
- ⚽ Upper body slightly bent.
- ⚽ Stretch for the ball with the arms.
- ⚽ Fingers held spread wide apart with the thumbs pointing inwards.
- ⚽ Control the ball after catching it, down on to the chest.

Mistakes
- ⚽ Not stretching out to use the arms when catching the ball.
- ⚽ Upper body not brought behind the ball.

2) Collecting (the ball)

Criteria
- Bring the body behind the ball.
- Legs are slightly bent.
- Fingers spread out wide.
- Upper body moves towards the ball.
- Collect up the ball and control it onto the chest.

Mistakes
- Hands and arms don't move to meet the ball.
- Legs are too wide apart.

Collecting up the low shot safely

3) Punching

Two-armed punch
- Fists held together on the inside surfaces.
- Broad backs of the hands are pointing slightly outwards.
- Run towards the ball and punch it out far.

One-arm punch
- Only use this as an exception.
- Punch with the surfaces of the fingers, not with the edge of the hand.

Mistakes
- Punching the ball downwards instead of upwards.
- Not moving towards the ball.

Punching save

Dive after the ball and deflect it away with one hand

4) Diving (after the ball)

Criteria
- Goalkeeper pushes himself off the ground.
- Tense the body.
- Catch, punch or deflect the ball in the air.
- Land on the side, hip or thigh.

Mistakes
- Hands not behind the ball.
- Body is not stretched out far enough.

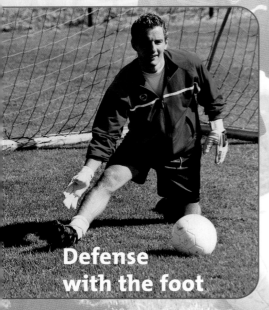

Defense with the foot

5) Foot defense

Criteria
- Kick the ball away as far as possible and out of danger.
- Deflect the ball to one side with one leg stretched out.

Mistakes
- Hitting to an opposing player.
- Too late with the foot block can lead to a collision i.e., foul.
- The ball is kicked out low.

6) Deflecting (the ball)

Criteria
- Used when the ball cannot be caught or punched away.
- Usually the body has to be fully stretched up.
- The ball is deflected using the inside of the hand or the fingertips.
- The deflection is made over the bar or to the side.

Mistakes
- The body is not stretched out enough.
- The power behind the shot is misjudged.

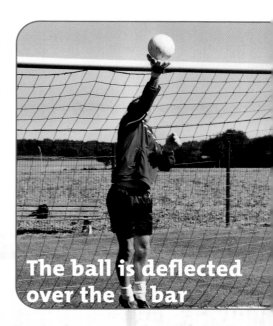

The ball is deflected over the bar

A) Goal kick

Criteria
- Ball is lying still on the ground.
- With or without a run-up the ball is brought back into play.
- The standing leg is next to the ball.
- Kick the ball in the middle with the instep.

Mistakes
- The standing leg is too far in front or behind the ball.
- The run-up to the kick is not timed correctly.

Kicking the lying ball

B) Kick out

Criteria
- The goalkeeper is holding the ball in the hands.
- Ball is tossed up slightly in front of the body.
- The ball is kicked with the instep as it falls.
- Remain exactly behind the ball.
- The kicking leg follows through.
- The upper body tips slightly backwards.

Mistakes
- The ball is tossed up too near to the body.
- The upper body is bent too far over the ball.
- The ball is not struck squarely by the instep.
- The whole movement is not smoothly executed.

The kick out from the hands

C) Throw out

Criteria
- The goalkeeper is standing slightly sideways to the direction of the throw.
- The shoulder is pointing in the direction of the throw.
- The opposite leg is in the forward position.
- The ball is thrown by the arm, sideways, from round behind the head.

Mistakes
- The goalkeeper is standing face on to the direction of the throw.
- The opposite leg is not placed forwards.

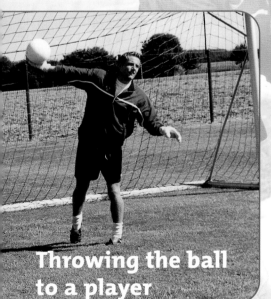

Throwing the ball to a player

D) Rolling pass

Criteria
- The goalkeeper rolls the ball flat to a player.
- The rolling pass is only recommended for short distances.
- Rolling the ball is done from a walking or running pace.

Mistakes
- The ball is rolled from hip height.
- A poorly rolled ball hops over the grass and causes the receiver to have difficulties controlling it.

Rolling the ball to a player

E) Passing

Criteria
- The goalkeeper plays the ball to a player with a foot pass.
- The passing movement is done flat with the inside of the instep.
- Over greater distances the ball is passed with a high ball.

Mistakes
- Lack of soccer skill qualities.
- Holding the foot wrongly.

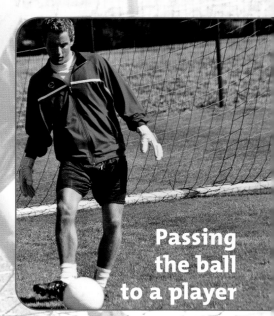

Passing the ball to a player

Positional Play

Good positional play makes it easier for the goalkeeper to successfully intervene in the game. In defense, correct positional play avoids risky maneuvers. In this way the goalkeeper can free another player out of a threatening situation by getting clear into a position to be able to receive a pass. On the other hand, good positional play can enable a speedy changeover to an offensive action by the home team.

In defense, the goalkeeper in modern soccer is increasingly faced with a one-on-one situation. Getting through this kind of situation is dependent largely on a lot of various experiences and not least a lot of training for it. Here are some possibilities for the goalkeeper:

- Run out to meet the attacker.
- Shorten the goal angle.
- Stand still.
- Wait for the attacker's next move.
- Concentrate only on the ball.
- Not react to the attacker's deceptive maneuvers.

Falling down has to be learned

More than often the goalkeeper ends his actions on the ground. A brilliant dive for the ball or fall should therefore be as "soft" as possible with a painless, safe landing following it up. Here are a few tips to lessen the fear of falling:

- For beginners, the goal mouth is hardly the best exercise spot because of the hard ground in that area. Sandpits or soft grass are better choices. However it is quite fun to fall down on a soft floor mat – ideal training equipment to constantly repeat the practice of fall techniques.

- When falling down from a kneeling position, low or high crouching position or from a standing position, the body rolls down over the lower leg, thigh and outside of the bottom. Don't land on the knees or the elbows!

- The falling movement, combined with catching or defending the ball away, is a complete, flowing movement sequence, which must be practiced until it is automatic and realizable at any time.

Keep alert!

Throwing the ball out with the hand

4 DEVELOPING CHILDREN'S AND YOUTH'S SKILLS

In order to be able to train children and youths properly, and in order to be able to fulfill the high expectations that children have with soccer, trainers have to learn about the important development features of children and learn how to implement these in training.

The development of a child does not follow a straight line of individual phases. There are many periods where growth and maturity go ahead in leaps and bounds. There are others where further development seems to stagnate. For some children these occur earlier on and for others a little later. They do not follow a straight line nor are they tied to age. Here, one could also look for the reason why children of the same age show considerable differences in their development. One also speaks of a biological age, in which physical development is measured, as well as a calendar age.

Knowledge of the way a child, or one who is growing up, develops is important, because each phase of the development has its own peculiarities. In certain phases, children and youths are more able to learn and react to particular stimuli. Training constructed with this in mind promises to be more effective. There are, for example, phases of development where power, stamina, speed or coordination can be exercised with a lot of success. In other periods of the development, for example, the acquisition of motor or technical skills can be encouraged.

The different development phases cannot be separated in a clear-cut manner, because the transition from one phase flows to another and each has its own individual features. Psychological research into development has come up with a number of step models.

In the following, a three-step model is suggested, because:

- On the one hand, it seems sufficiently discriminating to be able to reflect briefly on the necessary, theoretical background.

- On the other hand, sufficient scope for practical implementation is given.

STEPS IN DEVELOPMENT

Age Development Step	Training Aim
5-10 years early school age or primary school	The all-rounder in goal and on the field! Everyone is a goalie sometime.
Boys 10-12/13 years Girls 10-11/12 years Pre-pubescent Later school age	I would like to be a goalkeeper!
Boys 12/13-14/15 years Girls 11/12-13/14 years Gaining height 1st phase of puberty	We want to improve our Soccer!
Boys from 15 years Girls from 14 years 2nd phase of puberty (adolescents)	Goalkeeper - a stalwart of performance!
Players over 18 years Goalkeeper - the backbone of his team! Performance counts!	

Main Training Points

A varied basic training, no particular positional training, familiarization with the ball, intensive coordination training, throwing and catching the ball, everyone is a goalkeeper and a field player, team training only.
Precursor of the 'golden age of learning' i.e., learning the rudiments by playing.

Best age to learn, training of techniques in playing both from exercise and game situations, beginning of specialization towards goalkeeping, learning and developing further the rudiments as a goalkeeper with the ball, mainly team training, only a few periods of specialist goalkeeper training, catching balls, kick outs and throw outs etc.

Variable training provided, very good age to master techniques and improve fitness, consolidation of techniques on a high motor level, mastering coordination, training with the team, specialist goalkeeper training.

Competition training, refinement of techniques, working up one's own style as a goalkeeper identity, high intensive coordination and fitness training, introduction of opposition players, deliberate correction of mistakes.

Competition training complemented by individual correction of mistakes, specialist training, team training in all possible kinds of situation imaginable.

4.1 GOALKEEPER – ALL-ROUNDER IN THE GOAL AND ON THE FIELD – CHILDREN AND JUNIORS (UP TO 10 YEARS)

As already said in the description of psychological development, in this age group the main emphasis lies in a varied, sports-motor, basic training. A varied exercise regime of running, catching and relay races, combined with climbing, jumping, rolling, running and playful movements encourages the general basic motor capabilities. The basic techniques in soccer are practiced, bit by bit in their rudimentary form, by constantly being occupied in playing with the ball. Coordination is also improved using this playful emphasis.

In this age group there is no specialization and selection of a goalkeeper position per se.

In the training session, each player gets to learn the basic skills of the goalkeeper – catching, throwing out and drop kicking, clearing with the feet, punching out etc. In this way, the field players experience the challenges of the goalkeeping job from the beginning. It will soon be clear that it is a myth that the worst player is the one who is put in goal. In the games, one can even keep changing over the goalkeeper.

On the other hand, this experience contributes to the goalkeeper gaining an understanding of play, effected by partaking in the games. He can place himself in a position facing game situations and think how the opposition would attack and how he would direct his defensive players – all tasks, which are required of a modern goalkeeper. Each 'field player' will then learn what the particular capabilities that a goalkeeper must have, so that he can operate to an optimum on behalf of the whole team.

In many specialist publications, a warning is often given about specializing too early. Most, if not all experts recommend that a player should be selected to play in the goalkeeper position first after he has reached 10 years old.

In this age group, training runs under the motto of being a varied, general exercise and movement regime with the aim particularly of schooling the coordination abilities and coming to terms with the sports equipment. For this, the form of playful activities, such as obstacle races, games of skill, rhythmical running and jumping exercises, basic forms of gymnastics and athletics, testing reaction games, relay races and many others, is best. Demands on the coordination ability are significantly important as this forms the basic prerequisite for the further development of the motor system. Children trained well in coordination, later drop to learning new forms of movement easier and more quickly. "Coordination skills are developed more intensively up to the beginning of puberty (11/12 years old)". (Hahn: Kindertraining (Training Children), page 74).

Training tips

- 🌐 The children get to know about different pieces of equipment such as all kinds of balls (tennis balls, soccer balls, footballs, volleyballs, medicine balls, water polo balls etc).

- 🌐 Little games are played which serve to improve the reaction senses, speed and balance.

- 🌐 Using transparent situations and games, the children are familiarized with basic techniques. Movements, which are technical in form such as dribbling, passing the ball, throwing, catching and punching the ball out are exercised using little games. All the players do these exercises, including those specific to the goalkeeper.

- 🌐 Besides using a soccer ball, a change is rung by using a broader palette of other types of sport such as games of running and romping around, working hand over hand along a suspended rope or piece of equipment and hopping and jumping games.

- 🌐 Fitness has no role for children of this age group. Their fitness is improved already by all kinds of activities and movements they undertake playing. In this category, speed, flexibility, reaction and coordination are automatically exercised.

- 🌐 The goalkeeper position is rotated through all the players in training and in games.

- 🌐 Because children love to move about, training should be intensive and varied. In this age group, too much is never enough – the children will take a break themselves when they need it.

- 🌐 Because of the self-centeredness of children, above all up to the age of 7/8 years it makes sense to train in small, manageable groups.

Goalkeepers need a wide angle of view
and a large radius of action!

4.2 GOALKEEPER – THAT'S WHAT I WANT TO BE! JUNIORS (AGED 10-14 YEARS)

Building on the varied training and coordination exercises in basics learned up until now, the improvement of game play and techniques takes priority. Exactly in this age group, the awareness of the psychomotor development principles, i.e., the biological development process, can be well recognized. Following primary stages, 10-14 year olds go through a further process of maturing.

This phase is known as pre-pubescence or late school child age. "In this phase, children grow at approximately the same rate both in height as well as breadth and also the child's organs match this rate of development. This results in the harmonic and flowing ability to move" (c.f., W. Maier: Leistungsfussball (Performance in Soccer), page 17).

Meinel & Schnabel (1978), in their book on movement, call this phase the best learning phase. "Movement actions are very rapidly, often spontaneously learned. Children in this age group don't think long about things, they simply go ahead and try out the movement sequences demonstrated. They are then able to master them in a very short time" (Bischops/Gerards: Handbuch für Kinder- und Jugendfussball (Handbook on Children's and Youths' Soccer), page 48).

On the basis of a varied schooling in coordination, the children learn new movement sequences after very few attempts. At the beginning of the age group and development phase, the question of who will be the goalkeeper soon crystallizes itself. In the 10-11 year old group, the young person is in the best learning phase for motor system actions. He learns spontaneously. Progress in the anticipation of his own team members' and opposing team players' movements, as well as those of the ball, put him, for the first time, well in the position of taking on the job of goalkeeper. The necessary rudimentary techniques, such as catching the ball, throwing, punching, diving for the ball, catching the ball in the air etc., are quickly learned.

Now, the player's wish to want to be goalkeeper begins to grow, so that he stands in goal enthusiastically with a firm belief in himself. On top of this he can now fulfill the specific tasks of the goalkeeper more reliably and more successfully. Requirements, such as controlling the penalty box area and moving out to meet an attacker at the right time, can now be judged better.

The goalkeeper is no longer just 'put' in goal.
He puts himself in goal.

In the 10-11 year old age group, goalkeeper training begins seriously. Goalkeepers from this age on are regularly schooled in specific goalkeeping training. Field player training, however, must not be neglected.

Training tips for 10-11 year olds

- The goalkeeper works first of all on the rudiments of all the technical elements. After this, the movements are continually refined by expert correction, so that his competence in the game improves.
- In this age, the anticipatory capabilities (ability to adapt to changing circumstances) improve, so that he can judge the flight of the ball and the actions being taken by his own players, and those of the other team, much better.
- Children learn very quickly on the principle of being shown something and copying it (learning by imitating). It is therefore important that the trainer is also able to demonstrate the actions of the goalkeeper.
- Goalkeeper training should be exclusively carried out on a grass surface. Only then is diving for the ball also any fun.
- Also, in this age group, the goalkeeper should play in other positions on the field so that he can continue to get an impression of the action sequences in the whole game.
- Slowly, the self-centeredness of the children wears off; thus they are more and more in a position to play fully with others together.
- The specialist training for this age group serves principally to improve the techniques learned, which with the aid of targeted correction can increase to cover eventually the absolute finer points of detail.

The first phase of puberty

Girls 11/12 – 13/14 years old
Boys 12/13 – 14/15 years old

With the onset of the first phase of puberty, there is a slow change of build. Steady growth in height indicates to the trainer the end of the most successful learning period for the child. Where a gain in height is rapid, there is an imbalance created between the torso and the length of the legs so that discordant movements appear. With the large increase in height, learning new movement sequences becomes more difficult.

In the technical area, the skill elements have now to be internalized. The introduction of newer technical sequences is difficult and not particularly recommended, because the progress of learning can be sometimes very limited. The considerable differences experienced in growing up have to be compensated for by a different kind of exercise training.

Training Tips for 11/12 – 13/15 years old

- The goalkeeper tries to internalize the techniques learned.
- With the increase in strength and speed, the techniques learned already are brought onto a higher level in the environment of the competition and in correlation with the ball and an opponent.
- In occasional special training, individual mistakes can be corrected.
- Flexibility, skill and coordination can continue to be practiced more intensely.
- The trainer should gradually bring youths on to carry their own responsibility and give them time and space to practice their own things.
- The players should be encouraged and motivated for their wishes by praise from and discussion with the trainer.
- The special training sessions now gain more importance than the case with the younger ages in the group. The skills and techniques learned are now firmed up, made more dynamic and internalized.

The goalkeeper – quick reaction on the line.
But first, with the right ideas and safe hands!

4.3 GOALKEEPER – A PERFORMER JUNIORS (AGED 14-18)

At the end of the first phase of puberty, the ability to coordinate improves. This is followed by the second phase of puberty, which lasts for the ages of between 15-18 years old – for girls this is one year earlier. A physical regeneration process takes place. The body fills out and the motor system functions more harmoniously again. The young persons experience their second 'golden age of learning'. In this phase, movement sequences and techniques can be worked on for performance.

Youths develop gradually into goalkeeper personalities. Besides the specific goalkeeper techniques regarding precision and increase in speed, tactical schooling becomes more the order of the day.

Training tips

- The trainer shows the youths under him respect and accepts them as individual personalities.
- The pupils are gradually given more and more responsibility.
- Recognizing the cognitive development of the player, the trainer carries out discussions with the goalkeeper and clarifies the tactics to be used.
- Schooling of the goalkeeper techniques now takes on a detailed form. They are now firmed up and automated.
- At this time the psychological schooling is put into place. The trainer is advisor and assistant and gives support for the goalkeeper's confidence.
- Schooling of the fitness components such as stamina, jumping ability, speed can be carried out in the form of special exercise training.
- The ability to cope with pressure in youths at the end of this period is only slightly less than in adults.
- The goalkeeper has arrived at the end of his time as a youth and has to now move up into the Seniors Class. Here, the trainer can also be of great assistance.

4.4 BACKBONE OF THE TEAM – SENIORS

Already, at a youthful age, the goalkeeper gradually displays characteristics of becoming a personality. In the transition into the Seniors Class, it is part of the trainer's tasks, to encourage this process with his personal attention.

On entering the Seniors' phase, the special status of the goalkeeper becomes noticeably more significant. A goalkeeper personality can certainly represent a firm backbone for the team. He can radiate positive, motivating encouragement to his fellow players both in the defense as well as the attack. While the organization of the defense is his main job (c.f., Foreword by Jens Lehmann), when he is in possession of the ball he becomes the first attacking player in his team.

The main emphasis of the goalkeeper's training is now covered with these aspects in mind. Goalkeeper training must now be integrated more and more into team training.

Only in this way can the specific tasks (organization of the defense, playing together with the defense in game and standard situations, practicing back-passes, building up a fresh attack etc.,) be worked on and firmed up. On top of this, individual training can firm up the techniques and he can additionally be put under pressure specifically as a goalkeeper in team training (fitness training).

The exercise program for the 14-18 year olds is also valid for the Seniors, perhaps increased in its quantitative and qualitative demands. Differences regarding speed in the game play and the energy put into the commitment, as well as the explosiveness of the technique, however, can be managed according to performance reached and level of player.

5 THE GOALKEEPER AND THE TEAM

The goalkeeper and his teammates are members of one team and follow the same, joint aim. By virtue of his position, however, the goalkeeper has tasks, which no other player on the field can fulfill. Above all, here it is all about the cooperation between field player and goalkeeper, which has to be worked on in training and firmed up. The diagram that follows clarifies the training elements that have to be inter-visible. It will be quite noticeable that, above all, the defensive players have to have a clear understanding with the goalkeeper. However, even for offensive play, the intervention of the goalkeeper sometimes leads to game deciding advantages.

Goalkeeper in a one-on-one situation with an attacking player

Goalkeeper training in game situations

Training with the whole team

Joint defense,
Game sense

Organization of
the defense

Individual training
with defense players

Individual training
with attacking players

Practicing standard
situations

Goalkeeper playing
as sweeper

GOALIE

Goalkeeper is the
first attacker

Back-passing to the
goalkeeper

Goalkeeper initiating
field play

Goalkeeper serves the
ball to the attack
forwards

6 BUILDING UP A TRAINING SESSION

By virtue of the rule concerning back-passes to the goalkeeper, in force for some years now, he requires to have also skills as a field player, which he should train for and improve. This new, requisite quality as both a defensive and an attacking player demand, of course, an accentuation in the training regime.

ORGANIZATION OF TRAINING

Individual Training	Training of Game Situations in front of the goal
⚽ With the reserve goalkeeper ⚽ With the co-trainer ⚽ With the trainer ⚽ With/against an attacker ⚽ With another team player	⚽ With the whole team ⚽ With/against parts of the team ⚽ Defensive/offensive

Depending on the emphasis being set, the build-up of the training session will have to be varied.

In the following, an attempt is made to construct a rudimentary sequence (guidelines) for the build-up of a training session with the goalkeeper. Starting with the general division into three of "Start, exercise emphasis, conclusion", the following is a possible pattern.

Warm-up

Aims
- ⚽ Improvement of the general preparedness of the organs for performance e.g., cardiovascular system.
- ⚽ Stretching exercises.
- ⚽ Emotional mood.
- ⚽ Prevention against risk of injury.

Content   Warming up exercises (approx. 10-15 minutes)
Gymnastics and individual running exercises with and without the ball, or with the reserve goalkeeper or trainer. Whole body exercises, sprints, arm exercises, jumps etc.

However, the goalkeeper can also take part in the team warm-up exercises.

Training emphasis

Aims
- ⚽ Improvement of the coordination capability.
- ⚽ Building and firming up the coordination movement pattern.
- ⚽ Practice, improve and firm up specific goalkeeper techniques or the tactical plan.
- ⚽ The training emphasis can be achieved individually or as a team.

Content ⚽ Emphasis on coordination and techniques (30-40 minutes).
⚽ Reaction exercises, coordination content, schooling of skills and flexibility.
⚽ Improvement of specific goalkeeper techniques such as diving for the ball, catching, punching etc., practicing goal shots.

This individual work can be done together with the trainer, co-trainer, and reserve goalkeeper or field player.

Play conversion

Aims
- Using the content of the main emphasis.
- Practicing specific goalkeeper techniques and tactics in game situations.

Content
- Competitive game training (20-40 minutes).
- Joint play and tactics with the whole team or parts of the team.
- Goal shot training, dribbling with a shot at goal, one-on-ones, organization of the defense, standard situations such as free kicks, corners, attack build-up, and goalkeeper playing as a field player etc.

This competitive play training can also be the main emphasis of the exercises and thus will take up considerable time in the training session (10-15 minutes).

Cooling down

After the exertions of the training session, a cooling down period should be made with loosening exercises. This can done at the same time as the trainer and individual players discuss things between each other (10-15 minutes).

Tips

If the guidelines of this plan are used, and where each of the training aims are adjusted to each section, the following should be noted:

- For the 5-10 year old group, no specific goalkeeper training is included. Each of them will be goalkeeper sometime. Instead, the main emphasis is on a varied, physical basic training.
- For the over 12/13 years old group, additional goalkeeper training can be included.
- For this, the training plan above can be useful. The goalkeeper, however, continues to train further with the whole team.
- As age increases, the specific goalkeeper techniques are practiced more intensively and the rudimentary skills are practiced, eventually in all their detail.
- As in any training session, goalkeeper training should start with a warming up session, which should be directed towards the main emphasis that will be laid down for the session.
- After the warm-up there is a period to exercise coordination, so that the physical and mental mood is brought to an optimum level for the main emphasis in training that follows. Coordination training, carried out when tired, is not effective.

⚽ At the same time as carrying out the coordination training, the technical side can be thought about, because in many technical processes, good coordination is required. Coordination training can take place separately before the technique training part.

⚽ This will make sense if other pieces of equipment are being used such as batons, hoops, obstacles etc.

⚽ Competition exercises follow on from the coordination and technical training. This is where the goalkeeper gets an opportunity to use what he has learned from his technical training in game situations. Here it is all about cooperating together with his defensive players, the improvement of his own field playing ability as well as initiating attack play etc.

In conclusion, it should be noted that competition games in training can be carried out directly following on from the warm-up session and coordination training.

EXERCISES

7 KEEPING OCCUPIED AS A FORM OF GOALKEEPER TRAINING

Not only during training, but also when getting ready for a game, the goalkeeper has often the opportunity to occupy himself usefully. This can take the form of warming up exercises, by carrying out other main things such as coordination exercises, practicing techniques and doing fitness training, as well as going through specific goalkeeper skills.

This kind of occupation relies on a high degree of personal responsibility. Besides this he requires to be able to look at the effectiveness of the exercises he does, and understand their points and be convinced about the usefulness of the exercises. He must also exercise self-criticism, because in this form of training and preparation for a game there is only limited opportunity to carry out corrections – at least only personal corrections. On top of this the whole team cannot be brought into this. Despite these limitations, occupying himself with these things can form a useful aspect in the training plan.

In the following, we cover several suggestions for exercising on ones own.

Individual work with the ball

Firming up defensive type play

- ⚽ Throwing the ball up in the air and catching.
- ⚽ Throwing the ball up in the air and jumping to catch it.
- ⚽ Tossing the ball forwards a little and catching it on the run.
- ⚽ Throwing the ball up in the air, do a 360° turn and catch the ball.
- ⚽ Throwing the ball up in the air, do a forward roll and dive for the ball.
- ⚽ Bouncing the ball with the left or the right hand on the spot, turning round each time 360°.
- ⚽ Bouncing the ball with the left or the right hand as you move forwards.
- ⚽ Bouncing the ball as you skip along or gallop sideways.
- ⚽ Tossing the ball up in the air and punching it up again several times.
- ⚽ Throwing the ball up in the air and kicking it as it comes down again.

Firming up offensive type play
- Dribbling the ball with the left or the right foot.
- Running forward and controlling the ball with the foot.
- Dribbling the ball, stopping, pulling the ball back with the foot and then dribbling off again in a changed direction.
- Dribbling the ball and changing speed and direction.
- Throwing the ball up in the air and taking it on the chest.
- Throwing the ball up in the air, checking it on the chest and letting it drop to the ground and taking it on with the foot.

Two goalkeepers occupy themselves together

- Throwing the ball at each other in different ways and catching.
- Throwing the ball sideways at each other.
- Catching the ball (high up or sideways) on the jump.
- Catching the ball thrown sideways by taking one or two sideways steps.
- Catching or deflecting bouncing goal shots taken close in.
- Saving the ball with the foot in a one-on-one situation.
- Saving the ball with the hand in a one-on-one situation.
- Reacting to close shots at goal.

Other types of balls can be used in these or similar exercises providing a particular aim is being followed. For example, when carrying out fitness and strength training, a medicine ball can be used to good effect. Alternatively, when doing coordination and reaction exercises, a football (rugby ball) also serves a good purpose.

Game play exercises

Two goalkeepers carry out self-occupying exercises in a game play manner.
- Two goalkeepers stand 20 meters apart in the center of the field and throw a soccer ball to each other. The catcher may only throw the ball back from the spot where he caught it. Which of the two can drive the other back to his goal line first?
- The same game as above can be done in different forms: one-handed throwing, two-handed throwing, drop kicking, goal kicking, kicking a standing ball etc.
- One-on-one both goalkeepers each stand in a goal mouth 10-20 meters apart. The ball is rolled towards the other goal in a one-handed throw, or kicked at the other goal. The ball is thrown up and headed towards the other goal. Goalkeeper 'A' throws the ball at Goalkeeper 'B' in a way so that the other can kick the ball on the volley at the other goal.
- In a one-on-one situation, the two goalkeepers challenge each other for the ball for a few minutes without using their hands.

**Warming up
with the team**

8 WARMING UP WITH THE TEAM

In the training exercises, later in this book, you will sometimes find a general, simple note that says, "Warming up with the team". Here it is up to the trainer how much he involves the goalkeeper. At this juncture, we lay out a few varied tips that are designed to help the trainer, with the proviso that it should always be remembered to adapt for the age and ability of the players.

We can state the following maxim: According to the trainer's aim, the goalkeeper can always be included in the warm-up phase, either in his defensive function (as a goalkeeper) or more often in his offensive function (as a field player).

- Each player, including the goalkeeper, has a ball. All dribble along changing direction constantly. As they dribble the ball, they kick the ball up and catch it, or they play the ball up and deflect it away to the side with the hands, or the ball is picked up, headed and caught again.

- In groups of four, including the goalkeeper, the ball is passed between them. While, for field players the ball is passed low down, for the goalkeeper the pass is lifted up either high or to the side. The goalkeeper should catch the ball or deflect it away to a teammate.

- In groups of eight, including the goalkeeper, the ball is passed between them in any manner. However, the ball is passed to the goalkeeper so that he can collect it up. He then throws it out immediately to another teammate.

- In groups of five, including the goalkeeper, the ball is kicked between them on the volley. The goalkeeper catches the ball and volleys this out to a teammate.

- In groups of three, including the goalkeeper, the two teammates try to dribble round the goalkeeper. He tries to tackle the ball away from them with his foot.

GOALKEEPER TRAINING

	Up to 10 year olds	10-12 year olds
Coordination	Catching, running, throwing, jumping, ball familiarization, games of skill, running games, climbing, gymnastics	Self-occupation with the ball, ball familiarization, exercises using both legs, reaction exercises, balance, ball techniques
Fitness	No fitness training, speed training is done in a playful manner, catching games, relay races	Speed training, competing against a partner, relay races, catching games, introduction of stretching exercises, getting used to warm-up drills
Techniques	Ball familiarization, self-occupation with the ball, no specific goalkeeping training yet, regularly takes part as a field player	Working on specific rudiments of goalkeeping, playing as a field player, saving shots form all distances
Tactics	From 9/10 years old begin learning basic tactics, learning to recognize space on the field	Tactics schooling as cognitive ability increases

12-14 year olds	14-18 year olds	Over 18 year olds
Specific goalkeeper and soccer skills coordination training	Goalkeeping coordination training correlated to technical game play	Goalkeeping coordination training combined with technical and basic game forms
Flexibility, skills, stretching exercises	Exerting goalkeeper exercises, jumping ability, speed and acceleration, exercises with a partner	Increase of concentration ability, improvement of the specific elements of game play
Improve one-on-one skills, improvement of game ability in goal and on the field	Technique exercises for competitive game play, firming up the concentration	Firming up and refining skills until internalized, development of own personal style
Technique and tactical exercises, games with uneven sides, positional play, discussions with the defense	Goalkeeper tactics, cooperation with the defense, initiating attacks	Coordination with the defense players, tactics in the offensive, controlling the fullbacks firmly

Bringing the body and the hands behind the ball

9 TRAINING AIM – "COORDINATION"

In most books about soccer, there is a plethora of explanations and definitions about the term "coordination". In general, it can be described as follows:

"Coordination is the interaction of the central nervous system and muscles of the body in order to be able to carry out a sequence of movements"

Coordination, in respect of the game of soccer, is the ability, together with the use of the ball, to execute soccer game activities and safely manage situations when threatened by one or more opposing players. Coordination thus determines to a greater degree the sporting technique. The more that the coordination ability is developed and mastered, the more a player can manage situations with the ball skillfully. The reverse is also true – well executed techniques produce better coordination. This fact makes it clear how fundamental the value of "coordination" is for sports and in particular soccer.

In coordination training, different forms of movement such as running, jumping, turning, falling etc., are combined together. Experts differentiate between simple and complex coordination. Different aims in coordination exercises are therefore set for certain age groups and development phases.

Up to 10 years old
Children are brought up to be as **'versatile'** as possible, where the play equipment **"ball"** (not exclusively a soccer ball) is the middle point.

10-14 year olds
By virtue of being at a good learning age, here, **soccer** and also specific **goalkeeper** skills, as content of the session, come over well.

14-18 year olds and Seniors
Coordination, to be managed as **'multiple coordination'** – also in difficult conditions – is now combined with fitness, where goalkeeping tasks, in the defense and on the attack, largely form the central point.

COORDINATION EXERCISES AND GAMES

Coordination exercises require the use of different kinds of equipment and types of ball. Legend for the following exercise games is on the last page of this book.

Exercise 1

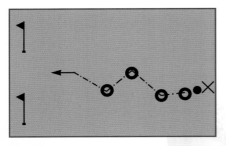

In front of a small goal mouth, four tires are laid down offset to each other. The player (here also the goalkeeper is a player) bounces the ball from tire to tire and after the fourth one throws/shoots the ball at goal.

Exercise 2

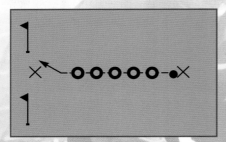

Five tires are lined up behind each other on the ground pointing towards a small goal mouth guarded by a goalkeeper. The player bounces the ball from tire to tire then lets it fall to the ground and dribbles towards the goal and shoots. He then replaces the goalkeeper and takes on his job.

Exercise 3

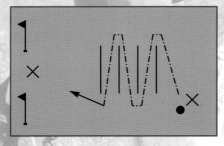

At distances of between 12 meters and 20 meters, several poles are laid on the ground crosswise to the small goal. The player dribbles through the slalom formed and takes a shot at goal. If the goalkeeper manages to hold the ball or deflect it, he stays in goal – if not – his place is taken by the scorer.

Exercise 4

Using ropes, a narrow corridor (60 cms) is formed in front of the small goal. Each player has to dribble the ball quickly through the corridor and at the end take on the goalie (1:1) and try and shoot a goal.

If the goalkeeper holds the ball he receives 2 points, if he deflects it he gets 1 point. If the shooter scores he gets 2 points. Each player has three goes.

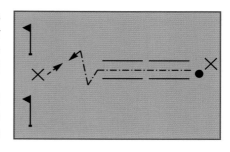

Exercise 5

The ball is rolled.
- The ball is rolled between spread legs.
- The ball is rolled through a figure of eight around the spread legs.
- The player rolls the ball forward, sprints after it and dives on to it.
- The ball is rolled between spread legs. The player does a complete turn round and dives after the ball.

Exercise 6

The ball is bounced on the spot.
- The ball is alternately bounced up high and then low.
- The ball is alternately bounced using the stronger hand and then the weaker one.
- The ball is bounced round the body to the left or the right.
- While the player is bouncing the ball he lies down and then stands up again.
- The player hops on the spot, bounces the ball with one hand while tracing a circle with the other hand.

Exercise 7

The ball is bounced on the move.
- While bouncing the ball, the direction is constantly changed.
- The player changes speed constantly while bouncing the ball.
- Hopping along, the player bounces the ball, turns round with his body and hops on further.
- The ball is bounced as the player runs backwards.

Exercise 8

Exercising throwing and catching the ball.
- The ball is thrown up at different heights and caught again.
- The ball is thrown up and caught on the jump.
- Using the right or the left thigh the ball is played into the air and caught again.
- From behind the back, the ball is thrown up over the head with both hands and caught.
- The ball is thrown up high into the air again and the player touches the ground with one hand before he catches the ball.
- The ball is thrown over the head from one hand to the other.
- From behind the back the ball is thrown high into the air, and after a quick turn round of the body, caught again.
- The ball is thrown up into the air backwards through the spread legs and after turning the body halfway round, caught again.
- Lying on the stomach, the ball is thrown up into the air and caught again. The ball may not touch the ground.
- Lying on the back, the ball is thrown up into the air and caught again or using an overhead kick played over the head.

Exercise 9

Field play skills are important for the goalkeeper.
- The goalkeeper practices dribbling with both feet.
- He dribbles the ball round cones, tires or over lines etc.
- He kicks the ball ahead and sprints after it.
- He kicks the ball ahead, sprints after it and dives on it.

Note:

If these exercises are done in a hall or gymnasium, a mat should be laid down as an underlay for the diving and falling exercises.

"Coordination ability – the basis for soccer"
Stefan Asmus

10 TRAINING AIM – "FITNESS"

When one speaks of goalkeeper fitness, one thinks of flexibility, reaction, speed, jumping ability and general upper body strength. The goalkeeper, in his zone of activity, must be able to stand up to the opposition and win through.

PROGRAM 1

Aim: Improvement of jumping ability

Exercise 1

Hopping over several small obstacles, such as balls, cones and other objects, is done together with a dive for a ball that has been thrown in. Afterwards the goalkeeper returns to his starting position as quickly as possible to begin the next series.

Exercise 2

The player jumps over a number of obstacles, which are lying behind each other. At each obstacle a ball is thrown at him hard and he has to catch it.

Exercise 3

After doing a forward roll the goalkeeper jumps in the air and catches a high ball, which has been thrown to him. He throws this directly back to the person who sent it and the exercise begins again.

PROGRAM 2

Aim: Improvement of jumping ability – with a partner

Exercise 1

Partner 'A' sits on the ground with his arms stretched out sideways. Using his left leg or right leg, Partner 'B' hops over the outstretched arm then hops over the outstretched legs and then over the other outstretched arm and continues round in a circle. From time to time, unexpectedly, Partner 'A' sitting on the floor throws up a ball which 'B' has to catch.

Exercise 2

Partner 'A' kneels arched out like a bench with his hands on the floor. Partner 'B' jumps over him and then crawls underneath and through the archway. Partner 'A' occasionally throws up a ball, which 'B' has to punch away.

Exercise 3

Both partners throw the ball at each other so that the receiver always has to jump for the ball.

Exercise 4

Both partners throw the ball at each other so that both the catcher and the thrower always have to jump for or with the ball.

PROGRAM 3

Aim: Improvement of speed and flexibility for basic goalkeeper drills in partner form

Exercise 1

The partners stand opposite and offset to each other 5-8 meters apart. Both have a ball, which they roll forwards with one hand. Just before they reach halfway, they change places and take on their partner's ball in the same direction.

Exercise 2

The partners stand opposite and offset to each other 5-8 meters apart. Each rolls his ball towards the other. In the middle each dives after the partner's ball.

Exercise 3

Using the starting position as above, the ball is played as a bouncing ball. Both players take on the partner's ball before it touches the ground for the second time.

Exercise 4

Partner 'A' and 'B' stand 10 meters apart from each other. 'B' does a forward roll, 'A' throws his ball up vertically while 'B' sprints for the ball, diving after it.

Exercise 5

'A' and 'B' stand opposite each other 10 meters apart. 'A' has two balls. The first ball he shoots in 'B's' direction. 'B' deflects the ball away, does a forward roll and deflects the second ball away, which has been thrown up high by 'A' by doing a stretched out dive to the side.

Exercise 6

In a boxed off area (penalty box) there are 3-6 balls. Both partners sprint from ball to ball and sit on each one. Whoever has sat on all the balls first, throws the last ball he sat on up in the air. This ball has to be caught by his partner before it strikes the ground.

PROGRAM 4

Aim: Strengthening exercises using the medicine ball with a partner

Both partners stand opposite each other 5-8 meters apart.
- The medicine ball is thrown between them and caught.
- The ball is thrown to the partner using one or two hands.
- The medicine ball is thrown and caught as a goalkeeper would a ball.
- The ball is thrown like a throw-in is done.
- The ball is thrown with one hand like a throw out, but in a manner that the partner can easily catch it.
- The ball is thrown up high and caught on a jump.
- The thrower turns his back on his partner and throws the ball as accurately as possible at him.
- The ball is thrown back immediately after it is caught.

In conclusion, it should be noted that these exercises can be done by any age group. They must be adapted, however, to account for the intensity of the exertion regarding development age and the performance ability of the soccer player. Because fitness work is mostly very exerting, appropriate time-outs should be planned.

11 THE GOALKEEPER BEFORE THE GAME

Regular training for the goalkeeper, by its very nature, serves as preparation for the competition game. Before the game, however, the goalkeeper needs a program, which is designed directly to get him into the right mood for the demands of the position.

Similar to the way training is constructed, the demands of a game require that proper game preparation be laid down as a premise. In this way the following demands can be met:

⚽ The warm-up program must be designed with the playing position in mind.

⚽ Defensive as well as offensive aspects from the goalkeeper's catalog must be taken into consideration.

⚽ In cooperation with the whole team or certain parts of it, group tactics can be gone through and practiced in warming up exercises.

Both hands behind the ball

AND HERE ARE THE EXERCISES...

General warm-up (8-10 minutes)

⚽ Loose trotting and running in different ways e.g., skipping, knees-up running etc.

⚽ Stretching of the muscle groups, which will be under strain in the exertions that follow.

⚽ Gymnastic exercises, also eventually with the reserve goalkeeper as a partner. Increased running exercises with and without the ball.

Warming up for specific positions (10-12 minutes)

In the following exercises we cover the basic techniques, which the goalkeeper should master:

- Catching goal shots and deflecting the ball coming in with flat, mid-height and high trajectories at the goal from different directions.

- Saving shots coming in after successful dribbling in a one-on-one situation.

- Flanking defense, with and without a threat from the opposition.

Simulation of game play (10-15 minutes)

When the goalkeeper has gained sure hands in mastering the basic techniques, he can now anticipate game situations. This form of work up can only be done with the team or parts of it.

- Five attacking players play against three defenders, so that the goalkeeper is intensively kept busy (sides uneven – plus in the attacking role; minus in the defender's role).

- High balls are kicked in at the goal area and these should be headed in by the attacking players. The goalkeeper has to be able to manage to save them all.

- In a game 3:3, the goalkeeper practices his field attacking play abilities.

This trilogy of warm-up and getting in the mood for the following competitive game takes into account the main important characteristics that a goalkeeper has to be able to master. Such an intensive warm-up program is not necessary for all age groups. This is particularly so for children's soccer. Systematic warm-up sessions start with the 10-12 year olds, since up until that age, it is only necessary to achieve a playful mood in the children before they start a game.

PREPARING FOR THE GAME – ALTERNATIVE PROGRAM

General warm-up (8-10 minutes)

- Loose trotting mixed with hopping, jumping and clicking the heels together, running sideways and stretched skipping.
- Individual work with the ball using the hands and the feet.
- Dribbling with the ball and bouncing the ball with the hand (alternate hands).
- Stretching of the muscle groups being used.

Warming up for specific playing positions (10-12 minutes)

- Shooting place shots at the goal to be saved by the goalkeeper.
- The ball is dribbled towards the goal and shot at goal from the penalty spot area.
- The goalkeeper has to save a goal.
- Using standard situations, the ball is shot at goal high up. The goalkeeper has either to catch the ball, punch it away or deflect it over the bar.

Simulation of game play (10-15 minutes)

- Four attacking players play against one defender plus the goalkeeper.
- Three attacking players play against the goalkeeper, but can only shoot at goal from outside the 16m box. Each time the goalkeeper holds the ball he has to throw it out to a player as accurately as possible.
- Corners are taken, which come in either low or high for two attacking players to shoot into goal. The goalkeeper has to try to intercept the ball. Each time he catches the ball, he kicks it with a low pass to the corner taker.

12 TEN TRAINING SESSIONS FOR CHILDREN (AGED UP TO 10 YEARS)

Once again, here are some points for trainers, exercise leaders or sports instructors to remember when they are teaching the youngest soccer players:

- Training should basically be of a playful nature.

- Having fun moving about, with and without the ball, must form the central point.

- Every player should be put in as the goalkeeper now and again.

- The goalkeeping basic techniques such as catching, throwing, diving after the ball and practicing falling down should be done in the form of games.

- Coordination training forms a central point in the training.

- While warm-up training is not necessary for this age group, it would not be wrong to get them used to such exercises.

- Because there is no firm goalkeeper chosen from this age group, the following exercise suggestions can be used for getting in the mood or warm-ups.

I can also catch the high balls

Exercise 1

Getting in the mood/Warming up

- Each child has a ball and moves around freely kicking it in an area 20m x 20m.
- If they run into another player, they sit down on the ball and then swap over balls with the partner.
- They roll the ball over the ground alternately using the right and the left hand.
- They throw the ball up high in the air. After jumping up several times they catch it again.
- They tap the ball on the ground and gather it up again as they fall down on the ground.

Exercise main emphasis

- The players are divided into three groups, hold hands and run round as a line.
- The running line stops and one player has a ball, which he throws to all the players one after the other.
- Then the ball is rolled to a player who plays it back to the sender with his foot.
- A 1m wide goal mouth is built. On each side of it, half of the players line up. One after the other, the ball is passed to the opposite side through the goal.
- Each player has a ball and may run around freely with it. Who can do a trick with the ball?

Game play

- Two teams of four players are formed. In a playing area of 15m x 15m there are two goals 5m wide guarded each by a goalkeeper. Each time a player scores a goal, he may change places with the goalkeeper as a reward.
- Four players form a team and practice penalty kicks at a 5m wide goal mouth. One of them is in goal for each round.

Exercise 2

Getting in the mood/Warming up

- In a space 20m x 20m, all the players run around with a ball each. Each player demonstrates all the tricks that he can do with the ball.
- When bouncing the ball lightly, it can be turned in the hands.
- The players spread their fingers of each hand out with the thumbs touching. The fingers are then relaxed.
- As they trot along, the players bounce the ball and try to get into a rhythm.
- The children touch hands with only the little finger of their hands, which they spread out. Then the hands are shaken into a relaxed position.
- The ball is thrown up into the air high and caught again using both hands.

Exercise main emphasis

- Each player chooses a partner and plays passing the ball with him. The passes can be thrown, kicked or headed to each other. The ball is always received by the hands. The ball is played to the partner either as a bouncing ball, a throw-in or a high ball pass. The partner always catches it with both hands.
- Six players form a circle. The exercise leader now calls out a name. This person has to receive a pass from whoever has the ball. This can be delivered either as a thrown or a kicked pass. The person named has to catch the ball.

Game play

- A little match is played with four players on each side. Each time a goal is scored, that team has to change over the goalkeeper so that each player gets a chance at being goalie. The goalkeepers have to concentrate on making sure they take the ball with their arms outstretched ('Get the ball!'). They then have to bring the ball with their hands onto their bodies ("It's my ball!"). When it is done correctly, the player is praised.

Exercise 3

Getting in the mood/Warming up

⚽ Two players partner up and have a ball between them. The player with the ball stands still while the other player runs round his partner, who keeps passing the ball out to him. The receiver has to catch or stop the ball while on the move, depending on how it is passed to him.

⚽ The standing player passes low balls to the running player using a shot with the side of the foot. The running player has to take on the ball on the move.

⚽ Both players run around passing the ball to each other.

Exercise main emphasis

⚽ Three groups of players are formed and line up for a relay race. The first player in each group does a split leg stance. The next player scrabbles through between the legs with the ball and shoots the ball back through the spread legs to the next player. He then joins in at the back of the group.

⚽ The second time the relay runs through, the ball is played gently back through the legs so that the receiving player has to throw himself after it.

⚽ On the third run-through of the relay, the ball is thrown back over the player so that the receiver has to reach for a high ball.

Game play

⚽ Two play against two with a goalkeeper in goal. Each team scores a point for each goal. Each time the goalkeeper saves the ball he also gets a point. Who has scored the most points in 5 minutes?

⚽ In the game 2:2 with a goalkeeper in the goal, the player who hasn't managed to score a goal after three shots has to go in goal.

UP

Exercise 4

Getting in the mood/Warming up

- All the players have a ball, which they dribble freely around the playing area. On a signal they stop the ball with the sole of the foot, sit down on it and then dribble it on further.
- The players dribble the ball describing a circle or a figure of eight. They do this with their stronger foot as well as their weaker foot.
- When dribbling along, the ball is stopped and then thrown up in the air and caught again using both hands.
- Standing still, the ball is thrown up high into the air. The player has to jump up once before he can catch the ball with a diving catch. A grass surface is required when doing this exercise.

Exercise main emphasis

- Teams of three are formed. One player stands as the goalkeeper in a goal 5m wide. The two other players stand about 6-8m away from the goal, one on each side of it. Each player may now shoot ten times at the goal – five with the left and five with the right. Who has scored the most points if each goal scores one point and each save also scores one point? Each player goes into goal once during the game.
- The three players form a triangle and pass the ball to each other in different ways. Each throw or kick is caught using the hands.

Game play

- Two teams of three players play against each other. There is no one person who is nominated as the goalkeeper. The goalkeeper is always the one nearest the goal when an attack is made by the other team.
- In a game of two teams with each three players, a goalkeeper is nominated. Each time a goal is scored he is replaced. The order of play is as per the player's first name.

Exercise 5

Getting in the mood/Warming up

- In the 16m area, cones have been dotted about. The players run around touching all the cones with their hands. Once they have done this they sit down.
- Each player dribbles round the cones with his ball. He must keep the ball close to his feet.
- The ball is being dribbled round the cones. Each time he reaches a cone he does a forward roll.
- The player dribbles round the cones again. When he reaches a cone, he rolls the ball through his spread legs, turns round quickly and dives after the ball.

Exercise main emphasis

- Teams of five players are formed. One player is placed in as the goalie. The four other players practice shooting a placed ball at the goal from a distance of about 7-10m.
- Each player has five goes at shooting and then changes over with the goalie.
- Using the same setup, in the second round of the game the ball is dribbled before shooting from a distance of 7-10m at the goal.
- Finally, in the third round the shots are taken with the ball rolling on the move.

Game play

- On each of the four sides of an area 20m x 20m, goal mouths 2m wide are set up using cones. Play is with 5:5. Saves may only be made using the foot and not the hand.
- Using the same field setup, this time play is with two balls. When an attack is being made, each player can act as goalkeeper and use his hands when standing on the goal line.

UP

Exercise 6

Getting in the mood/Warming up

- A "forest of cones" is laid out in an area 15m x 15m. The players dribble the ball through the 'forest' without touching a cone. If a player touches a cone he has to throw the ball up in the air three times and catch it with both hands.
- This time the players bounce the ball through the 'forest'. If they lose the ball or touch a cone, the player has to roll the ball through his legs, turn round and dive after the rolling ball.
- The players roll the ball through the 'forest of cones'. At each cone they have to go round it once, bouncing the ball with their hands.

Exercise main emphasis

- Groups of six are formed and they stand in a semi-circle. One of the players positions himself in front of each group and throws the ball at the members in the group.
- Throws are done first of all at chest height, then head height and then at knee height. The thrower is changed over after each round.
- The thrower is throwing the ball at the other players as before. They have to clap their hands twice before they catch it.
- The thrower delivers balls as high up as possible. As he does this he calls out the name of a player who has to catch the ball.
- The thrower calls out two names. These players have to challenge each other to be the first one to touch the ball after it has landed on the ground from a high throw.

Game play

- A game of tag is played using the ball to hit the other players. Each player struck by the ball goes into the middle to join the 'King' and has to stay there. The target area is the whole body. A 'tag' which touches the ground before striking a player is also valid. Only players who manage to catch the ball can play on.

Exercise 7

Getting in the mood/Warming up

- "Shadowing": Two players are a team. Both players have a ball. The leading player does various exercises with his ball (e.g., dribbling, bouncing the ball, and throwing the ball up in the air), which the follower-on has to copy.
- This time the leading player doesn't have a ball and changes direction often as he runs along. The follower-on has to copy the changes carrying his ball.
- Both players run along with one of them about 3m behind the other. The follow-on player has a ball. On a signal the first player stands still with his legs spread out. The second player throws the ball through the other's legs and he has to dive after the ball and try to capture it.

Exercise main emphasis

- In order to exercise reaction, two players play "stealing the ball" with each other. One player has a ball and plays around with it as he feels fit. The partner's task is to try and 'steal' the ball away from him using fair means. If he is successful, roles are changed over. Players are not allowed to take more than five paces with the ball in the hands.
- Partner 'A' passes the ball in different ways to Player 'B', who has to catch the ball or at least touch it.

Game play

- Two teams play against each other – each player has a number. When a player scores a goal, he and the player with the same number in the opposing team, replace the goalkeeper on their respective side.
- The same teams play against each other, but this time, goals scored are pointed with the number of the player who scored the goal. After each goal is scored, the scorer can chose who should go in goal.

Exercise 8

Getting in the mood/Warming up

- In a marked-off area, the players dribble round with the ball at their feet. On a signal by the trainer, they push the ball forward a little and dive after it. They gather the ball up and pull it into their body for protection.
- The players throw the ball high up in the air, quickly do a forward roll and dive after the bouncing ball.
- Catch the donkey's tail: The players move around in a marked-off area with a ribbon or length of paper tucked into the band of the shorts. On a start signal each must try to grab as many 'donkey's tails' as possible, without losing their own.

Exercise main emphasis

- Two players have a ball, which they throw to each other and catch.
- The ball is dropped from hip height and passed to a partner using the instep of the foot.
- Throw the ball at a partner so that he can head it back.
- When playing about with the ball with a partner, each player must throw it back from the spot where he gathered it up or caught it.

Game play

- Tiger ball: Using a marked-off playing area 20m x 20m, all the players dribble the ball around. One player is the 'Tiger' and tries to get the ball off another player as a goalkeeper would. After one minute the 'Tiger' is replaced.
- Left-footed soccer – this could be so for most of the players. Two teams play against each other, however the ball may only be played using the weaker foot. If, for example, a goal is scored using the stronger foot, this doesn't count.

Exercise 9

Getting in the mood/Warming up

- Two teams standing 3m apart form a corridor along the center line. The trainer rolls the ball along the ground down the corridor. Everyone plays as goalkeeper and dives after the ball.
- The ball is thrown along the corridor at medium height. All the players try to catch the ball or fist it away.
- The ball is thrown along the corridor at just above head height. The players have to touch the ball or deflect it away.

Exercise main emphasis

- The teams line up for a relay race opposite each other. The ball is kicked at the man standing opposite, then dribbled and finally kicked as a shot at goal.
- Both teams stand with legs spread out opposite each other. The first player dribbles the ball through the open legs of the opposite team. At the end is a player waiting to pick up the ball with both hands. He then places the ball down in front of him and dribbles the ball to the opposite team and the second round begins the same way.
- Team 'A' stand representing slalom poles for Team 'B' to play through with the ball at the feet. The 'slalom poles' can of course wave about, but one foot must remain firmly on the ground. They can try to kick the ball away from the slalom runners.

Game play

- Two teams of four play against each other in a small playing area with a goalkeeper. If the goalkeeper can stop a shot at goal, he changes places with the shooter. The shooter goes into goal, while the last goalkeeper takes up a position as a field player in the other team.
- Two players play against a small goal mouth with a goalkeeper. Each time the duo score a goal they gain one point. Each save by the goalkeeper earns him one point. Who can reach 10 points first?

Exercise 10

Getting in the mood/Warming up

- Each player has a ball, which they throw forward and sprint after until they catch up with it and stop it with the sole of the foot.
- The players lay the ball forward and try to overtake it.
- They place the ball on the head, let it drop down, turn themselves round and catch it.
- The players throw the ball high up in the air, run through underneath it and dive after the bouncing ball.
- The players throw up the ball a short way, head it and catch it again.

Exercise main emphasis

- Pairs of players trot forward slowly, passing the ball between them.
- In a slow trot, the ball is thrown to the other so that he can safely catch it.
- One player kicks the ball into an open area. Both sprint after it and tackle each other to gain possession.
- The player in possession of the ball tries to out-dribble his partner. If he loses the ball then they change roles.
- One player lets the ball fall out of his hands onto the ground and shoots it across to his partner.

Game play

- Play is with 3 against 2 plus a goalkeeper. While the team of three is always attacking, the defending goalkeeper and his two players are always defending. Each save done by the defending team earns them one point, but the attacking team gain two points for a goal.
- Play is 3 against 3 and each team has to nominate a goalkeeper. Goals scored by field players count as normal, while if a goalkeeper scores a goal, his team gets 3 points and the goalkeeper is replaced by a field player.

10-12

13 TEN TRAINING SESSIONS FOR JUNIORS (AGED 10-12 YEARS)

Once again, to begin with, for the trainer, exercise leaders and sports instructors here are a few reminders about what to think about for this "golden age of learning" phase.

- As before, schooling of the coordination is very much the central point of emphasis for training.

- Training includes, once again, numerous playful elements, which should mask out the monotonous character of the exercises.

- Gradually, a goalkeeper is emerging from the circle of players. Within the team, he shows a particular interest in this playing position.

- The goalkeeper now takes the path of going from the basic learning of technical skills such as throwing, catching, diving after the ball etc., through to the finer points. This process is, however, a slow one.

- The beginning of tactics training is started with tasks such as playing in different positions, mastering standard situations and the opportunities of building up the game play by the goalkeeper.

- Realization of the necessity of warming up sessions is brought home to the players along the principle of habit.

- As before, work on the playing field must be fun for the players, and this is the best kind of motivation.

In the following, there are five training exercise sessions for individual work as a goalkeeper, and five for training with the team or parts of the team.

In the training sessions, which are constructed using the participation of the team, the aspect of "getting in the mood/warming up" is only coincidental, since in this phase, the goalkeeper can do the warm-up together with the whole team.

Exercise 1 INDIVIDUAL TRAINING

Aims

- ⚽ Catching and saving straight shots at goal.
- ⚽ Getting used to the ball.
- ⚽ Schooling of coordination.

Training partner

Trainer/Co-trainer.

Getting in the mood/Warming up

The goalkeeper has a ball.
- ⚽ He dribbles the ball with his left and right foot.
- ⚽ He takes the ball in the hand, throws it up high and catches it again.
- ⚽ He throws the ball high up in the air and as it falls, he kicks the ball forward and up again with his knee and dives after it.
- ⚽ The ball is bounced with the right and then the left hand.
  Galloping sideways, the ball is bounced with alternate hands.

Exercise main emphasis

Starting with coordination schooling exercises using hoops.
- ⚽ Nine hoops are laid in a line. Run down the line – the ground may only be touched once inside each hoop.
- ⚽ The stepping space between hoops is made smaller, so that two steps may be taken inside each hoop.
- ⚽ Every second hoop is removed. When running through the hoops, the right foot is placed inside the hoop and the left leg is put down between the hoops. Then do it with the opposite feet.

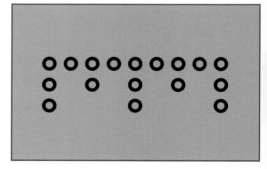

- Three hoops are left lying on the ground. When running through the line of hoops, each time the right foot is put down it has to be inside a hoop.
- Nine hoops are laid out again. When running down the line of hoops, a ball is tossed from the right hand into the left hand and back again.
- The ball is bounced down the line of hoops. The ball should only be bounced once in each hoop.
- At the end of the line of hoops the goalkeeper bounces the ball forwards and dives after it.
- At the end of the line of hoops, which the players run through without the ball, the trainer throws a ball sideways into the running direction and the goalkeeper dives after it.

Game play

- The ball is thrown by the trainer/co-trainer and caught by the goalkeeper, who throws it back straight away. How many passes like this can be done in 30 seconds?
- The trainer shoots at goal using a drop kick. How many of these can the goalkeeper save?
- The trainer throws awkward bouncing shots. How many of these can the goalkeeper save?
- In conclusion, the goalkeeper plays a game with the whole of the team or parts of it.

10-12 YEARS

Exercise 2 INDIVIDUAL TRAINING

Aims

- Falling down sideways and saving low balls.
- Schooling of coordination.
- Getting used to the ball.
- Practicing the clearing throw with the hands.

Training partner

A second goalkeeper

Getting in the mood/Warming up

Both goalkeepers have a ball.
- Moving along the ball is bounced with the right/left hand alternately.
- The ball is carried in the hands when running about. The player then goes into a squatting position and rolls over the hip sideways. This exercise is done to the left and the right.
- The goalkeeper chooses between adopting a kneeling or a squatting start position.
- The partner throws low balls at his right or left side. The goalkeeper rolls down over his hip and saves the ball.

Exercise main emphasis

- A path is erected using poles or cones. The goalkeeper has to run through the line. At each marker, the goalkeeper squats down and rolls over sideways.
- The previous exercise is repeated. The partner is standing at the last pole/cone and rolls a ball at the goalkeeper, either to the left or the right from the side. The goalkeeper has to save or catch the ball by rolling sideways.

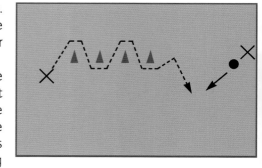

- The goalkeeper runs through the line of poles/cones. At the end, his partner kicks a low pass to him, which he has to get hold of by rolling and falling.

Game play

- The goalkeeper is standing in the goal mouth and carries out clearances by throwing the ball as far as possible to a partner up the playing field. The partner collects the ball with his foot, dribbles towards the goal and shoots a low shot at the right or left corner of the goal. After a while, they change over roles.
- The partner now throws the ball at the goal as for a throw in. The goalkeeper has to save such high balls. As before, they change over roles after a while.
- The partner runs with the ball at his feet towards the goal and tries to dribble round the goalkeeper. He tries to save the ball or take it away from the partner by falling sideways to get the ball.

10-12 YEARS

Exercise 3 INDIVIDUAL TRAINING

Aims

- ⚽ Getting used to the ball.
- ⚽ Schooling of coordination.
- ⚽ Diving sideways and catching medium height balls.

Training partner

Trainer/Co-trainer.

Getting in the mood/Warming up

The goalkeeper has a ball.

- ⚽ He dribbles the ball using the left or the right foot.
- ⚽ The ball is bounced with the left or the right hand. He does this while running in smaller or larger circles.
- ⚽ On the move, the ball is thrown up as high as possible and caught by jumping up towards it.
- ⚽ Doing a loose trot, the ball is thrown up in the air, then headed and caught again. A high ball is caught, thrown a little to the side and a dive made to grab it.

Exercise main emphasis

- ⚽ The goalkeeper is standing in goal and his partner throws medium height balls to his right or left side. At first, the side being thrown at is announced before the throw. Later this is left out and the goalkeeper has to anticipate which side the ball will come in at after it has been thrown.
- ⚽ The goalkeeper stands in a squatting position and tries to catch or deflect the balls coming in down the side.
  From a standing position, the goalkeeper has to dive to stop the balls thrown at medium height.
- ⚽ The partner tries to trick the goalkeeper on which side he will throw the ball.

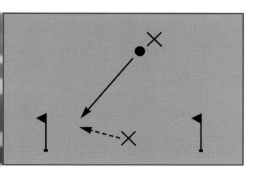

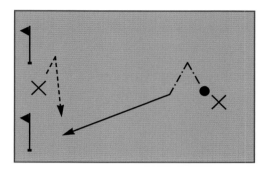

Game play

- When the goalkeeper and the trainer are playing the ball to each other, it must be thrown on again from the spot where it was caught. The goalkeeper must always use a clearing throw and throw it exactly in the direction of the trainer.
- The same game can be played using the kick out, in which case the goalkeeper and the trainer must be further apart.

10-12 YEARS

Exercise 4 INDIVIDUAL TRAINING

Aims

- ⚽ Catching high balls.
- ⚽ Doing spot kicks.
- ⚽ Schooling of coordination.
- ⚽ Getting used to the ball.

Training partner

Trainer/Co-trainer.

Getting in the mood/Warming up

- ⚽ The ball is played between the trainer and the goalkeeper. While the goalkeeper always plays the ball to the trainer as a low ball, the trainer's passes, which the goalkeeper has to catch, are always carried out differently.
- ⚽ The goalkeeper throws the ball up high and jumps up after it, catches it and throws it to his partner.
- ⚽ The partner throws high balls at the goalkeeper, who has to run after them and catch them with a jump.
- ⚽ The goalkeeper throws the ball up as high as possible into the air, twists quickly round in a circle and then jumps up towards it to catch it.

Exercise main emphasis

- ⚽ The partner throws high balls straight in front at the goalkeeper.
- ⚽ The trainer drop kicks the ball high at the goalkeeper, who has to catch it.
- ⚽ The partner throws the ball high to one side of the goalkeeper, who has to take one or two steps to catch it.
- ⚽ When throwing the ball up high, the partner doesn't indicate to which side he will throw the ball. The goalkeeper has to anticipate which side it will come in at after it has been thrown.
- ⚽ Two flat obstacles are placed on each side to the right and left of the goalkeeper, which he has to avoid before he can catch balls thrown in to his side.
- ⚽ The goalkeeper does a forward roll, after which his partner throws him a high ball to catch down one side.

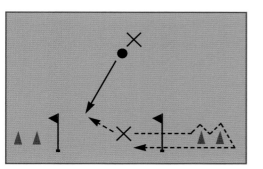

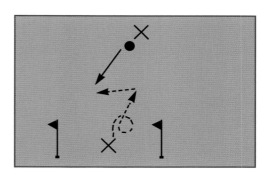

Game play

- The goalkeeper carries out a kick out from the spot. The trainer collects the ball up with his feet, dribbles a few meters and shoots in the direction of goal down one side.
- The goalkeeper has to carry out kick outs from the spot at different distances in such a manner that they land in a marked-off area 5m x 5m.
- The trainer and goalkeeper play low balls to each other. These should be reasonably accurately placed so that they land at the partner's feet. As they play, each step that one of them has to take to reach the ball counts as a minus point. Who ends up with the least minus points?

10-12 YEARS

Exercise 5 INDIVIDUAL TRAINING

Aims

- Firming up the basic techniques.
- Schooling of coordination.
- Improvement of the feel for the ball.

Training partner

Field player/striker.

Getting in the mood/Warming up

- Goalkeeper and partner practice passing low balls on the move.
- The striker kicks the ball at the goalkeeper in different ways. The goalkeeper tries to bring the ball under control as quickly and as safely as possible. He then rolls the ball out to the striker again so that he can play it at goal again.
- The goalkeeper throws the ball out to the striker – starting at short distances and then at longer distances. The striker stops the ball and dribbles it towards the goalkeeper and tries to get round him. The goalkeeper tries to get the ball off the striker.

Exercise main emphasis

- The goalkeeper stands in the goal and the striker shoots the ball differently from a spot kick at goal – low/half-high/from the frontal position and from a side position.
- The striker keeps changing his shooting position by varying distances and angles.
- In a 1:1 situation, the striker dribbles the ball towards goal. The goalkeeper has to try to either save the shot or at least to touch the ball with one hand.
- The striker kicks the ball at goal from the 5m area using easy low shots. The striker may try to trick the goalie, but the ball must not pass the goalie by more than one meter.

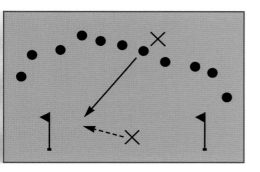 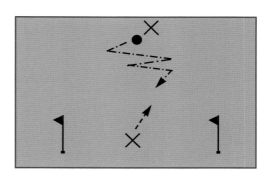

Game play

- In a 1:1 situation, the goalkeeper and the striker play kicking at two small goal mouths. Hands may not be used.
- In a 1:1 situation, the goalkeeper and the striker play against each other. While the goalkeeper defends a proper goal mouth and may use his hands, he has to score against two small goal mouths, which the striker, however, can only defend using his feet. Who wins?
- Playing against two small goal mouths, the striker and the goalkeeper play as both field player and goalkeeper. If the goalkeeper shoots a goal he gets 2 points, but the striker only gets one point. If the striker saves a goal he gets 2 points, however the goalkeeper gets only one point for a save.

10-12 YEARS

Exercise 6 TEAM TRAINING

Aims for the goalkeeper

- Getting used to the ball.
- Saving long shots.
- Throwing the ball out to a team player.

Aims for the field players

- Executing long place shots.
- Improvement of ball control.
- Collecting up balls thrown at them.

Getting in the mood/Warming up

The goalkeepers take part in the warm-up for main emphasis play together with the team. This can be done in the form of individual ball work for example.

Exercise main emphasis

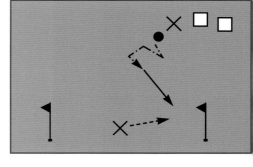

The field players dribble with the ball towards the goal and execute long shots from a distance, which the goalkeeper has to save where possible. When he has got the ball under control, he throws it out again accurately to the field player.

- The run at goal is done down the middle.
- The field players run diagonally at goal from one side.
- The players run at goal alternately from the left and the right diagonally at the goal so that the goalkeeper has to reorient himself after each shot.
- The players dribble the ball across and parallel to the goal mouth and shoot out of a turn. This is practiced both coming in from the right and the left side.

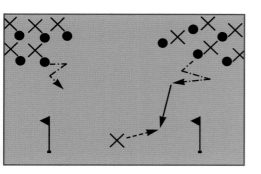
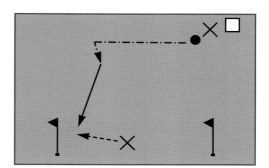

Game play

 Play is carried out at a goal mouth defended by a goalkeeper. Five attackers play against three defenders (situations with outnumbered/superior numbers), so that many shots at goal are achieved. For this, the attackers have to use long shots. The goalkeeper throws saved shots back out to a player in the attacking team.

As an addition to the above game, the defenders play at two goal mouths made from poles.

10-12 YEARS

Exercise 7 TEAM TRAINING

Aims for the goalkeeper

⚽ Saving flanking shots.
⚽ Saving long shots.
⚽ Getting used to the ball.

Aims for the field players

⚽ Accurate flanking shots.
⚽ Improvement of ball control.
⚽ Placed shots from a distance.

Getting in the mood/Warming up

The warm-up is done with the whole team. This time it is carried out as games by holding several different relay races, and in the second part more in a competitive form.

Exercise main emphasis

⚽ The player stands near the sideline and dribbles towards the goal line. Shortly before reaching the goal line they cross the ball from the flank at the goal mouth. The goalkeeper catches the ball and throws it out to a field player, who dribbles towards the goal again and shoots from a sharp angle at goal. This exercise is practiced from both sides of the goal mouth.

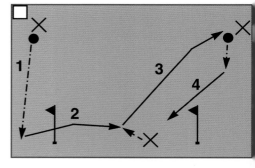

⚽ The game above is repeated. This time, however, as the goalkeeper catches the ball coming in from the flank, he is harassed gently by a player standing in front of the goal. The goalkeeper has to ensure he takes the ball as safely as possible and bring the ball firmly under control.
⚽ The flanking shots at goal are taken from spot kicks on the goal line. The goalkeeper has to catch the ball and immediately throw it out to a field player, who is positioned some 15-10m in front of the goal. He shoots the ball at goal with a long shot, so that the goalkeeper has to react quickly again.

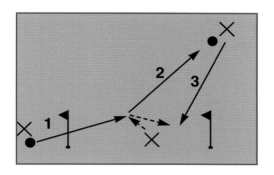

Game play

Two teams play at two goals. Each time a goal is scored from a flanking shot, it earns two points. Each goal saved by the goalkeeper following a flanking shot earns the goalkeeper's team two points.

Exercise 8 TEAM TRAINING

Aims for the goalkeeper

- Improvement of goalkeeping skills.
- Getting used to the ball.

Aims for the field players

- Improvement of ball control.
- Practicing basic techniques such as passing and dribbling.

Getting in the mood/Warming up

The team, including the goalkeeper, warm up together. This time, emphasis is on short sprinting. This allows all kinds of catching games to be played – with or without the ball.

Exercise main emphasis

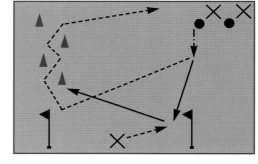

- The players dribble towards the goal from the center line, one after the other and pass the ball to the goalkeeper. He takes the ball in both hands and throws it back to the player, who collects it up with his feet and dribbles it through a slalom course back to the center line.
- From the center line, the players dribble towards the goal and pass the ball to the goalkeeper. He collects the ball up with his feet and kicks it back to a teammate, who, in turn, kicks the ball with a long shot back into the center circle.
- The players dribble towards the goal from the center line and pass the ball at a medium height to the goalkeeper. He tries to get the ball under control without using his hands and passes it back to the person who passed it to him. This person, in his turn, passes the ball back to the center line so that it comes to a rest as near as possible to it.
- From the center line, the players dribble towards the goal and try to score a goal. Whoever kicks wide, or whose shot the goalkeeper saves, has to repeat the exercise.

Game play

Two goal mouths are positioned about 40m apart. There is a goalkeeper in each goal. A pair of players is about 10m in front of the goal. A third player throws a high ball into the goalie, who has to punch it clear over the two players. Both players try to get possession of the ball and then 1:1 against the goalkeeper, score a goal.

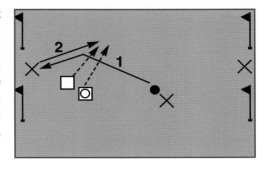

10-12 YEARS

Exercise 9 TEAM TRAINING

Aims for the goalkeeper

- Improvement of catching techniques.
- Learning about positional play.
- Getting used to the ball.

Aims for the field players

- Improvement of ball control.
- Structuring combined play.
- Practicing goal shots.

Getting in the mood/Warming up

The goalkeeper warms up with the team. Various passing combinations are practiced in pairs.
It is important that all players are kept on the move all the time and often have to sprint after the ball every now and again.

Exercise main emphasis

- The goalkeeper takes up his post in goal, while all the pairs of players pass the ball to each other in the center of the field. When the trainer signals, one pair come forward towards the goal passing to each other and end up the run by shooting at goal.

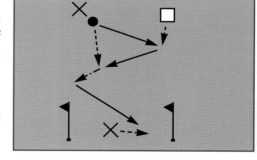

- The pairs move around in the center of the field, passing between each other. On a signal, both players, kicking the ball, run in the direction of the goal. The player in possession of the ball plays it outwards. From this point the other player kicks it back into the center, where a goal shot is carried out.

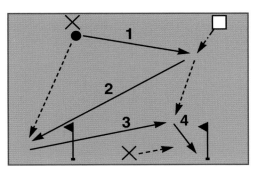
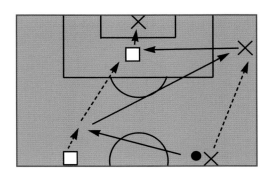

⚽ A pair of players starts out from the center line towards the goal, passing the ball between themselves. One player kicks the ball sideways to his teammate, who then flanks the ball back diagonally in, where it is either headed or kicked on the volley at goal.

Game play

⚽ In the center of the one half of the playing field, two goals are erected back to back, with a goalkeeper positioned in each goal mouth. Teams of 5:5 or 6:6 circulate round playing at the two goals. Each team can shoot at either goal.

⚽ Start as in the game above, but this time each team has to shoot at his opposing goal.

⚽ In the same game as above, this time both goals are guarded by only one goalkeeper. He has to keep changing his position.

10-12 YEARS

Exercise 10 TEAM TRAINING

Aims for the goalkeeper

- ⚽ Schooling of coordination.
- ⚽ Firming up the basic techniques.

Aims for the field players

- ⚽ Practicing shooting skills.
- ⚽ Improvement of ball control.
- ⚽ Improvement of combined passing moves.

Getting in the mood/Warming up

The goalkeeper gets into the mood together with the team. All the players dribble the ball around in a 40m x 40m playing field area. The trainer calls out a player's name and he has to immediately play the ball to the goalkeeper.

- ⚽ The ball is played low to the goalkeeper so that he can collect the ball up.
- ⚽ The ball is played hard at the goalkeeper so that all he can do is to save it.
- ⚽ The ball is played in high so that the goalkeeper has to catch the ball before he rolls it out again to the player.
- ⚽ The ball is played in from the side so that he has to chase the ball and dive after it.
- ⚽ The goalkeeper has to take on the role of a field player.

Exercise main emphasis

Two goal mouths are positioned on the playing field at a distance of about 40m from each other.

⚽ Each player dribbles his ball towards Goal 'A' and tries to deliver a long shot at goal. The goalkeeper catches the ball and throws it out to the player as he is on the move. He has to run through a slalom course in the direction of Goal 'B', where he delivers a flanking shot to be caught by the goalkeeper standing there.

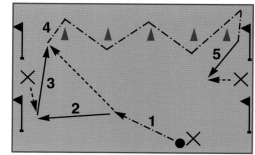

- On the second run through of the same game, however, the person doing the flanking shot is additionally 'hindered' by a defender.
- On the third run through of the same game, a defender hinders the person dribbling towards the goal. The attacker has to play round the defender, without giving him the opportunity to chase after him.

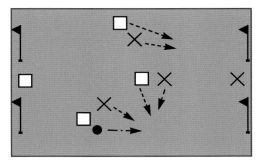

Game play

- A tournament is played on a half-pitch with 3 and a goalkeeper against another 3 plus goalkeeper. Goals may only be scored by using low shots, while the goalkeeper is only allowed to defend with his feet.
- In a similar game on a half-pitch, the player at the rear becomes the goalkeeper. This means that goalkeepers get to play as field players.

10-12 YEARS

Catching a high ball with a safe jump

12-14

14 Ten Training Sessions for Juniors
(AGED 12-14 YEARS)

Once again, as a summary, here are a few reminders about what aspects to think about for this phase for Juniors aged 12-14 years.

- Basic techniques – throwing, catching, diving after the ball etc., – all which a goalkeeper has to master, have to be worked on and perfected further.

- Now, the goalkeeper's actions, when building play up such as clearance kicks, goalkeeper's kick out, clearing passes, have to be perfected.

- Similarly, the schooling of coordination always has its place firmly on the training program.

- In tactics training, the goalkeeper now also has to think about the organization of the defense.

- The inclusion of stretching exercises during warm-ups can be easily brought home to players in this age group.

- Similarly, power training now plays a role, but nevertheless by using games in a playful manner.

- It becomes clear to these youngsters growing up that, for the first time, a certain amount of responsibility for themselves and their performance is required, and this plays a big role in the whole team's game.

- Preparation for training and the game, but also for cooperation within the team, becomes increasingly stronger as an aspect of individual responsibility in the mind of the player.

YEARS

Exercise 1 INDIVIDUAL TRAINING

Aims

- Getting used to the ball.
- Catching and saving straight frontal shots.
- Improvement of goal line reaction.

Training partner

Trainer/Co-trainer

Getting in the mood/Warming up

The goalkeeper keeps busy with the ball and is always on the move.

- In a loose trot, he bounces the ball with the right and the left hand. Every now and again he does quick sprints over about 10m.
- He throws the ball high up in the air and catches it on the jump.
- He throws the ball up high, deflects it away with his hand and dives after it.
- The ball is held tightly between the feet and whipped up and caught again.
- He throws the ball up high, does a forward roll and then catches the ball again.
- Dribbling the ball along, he dodges and weaves, changing direction.
- He invents some tricks with the ball, which he keeps practicing.

Exercise main emphasis

About eight poles are laid down offset about 1m apart behind each other.

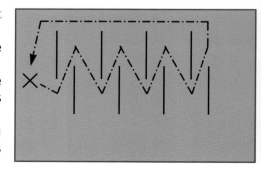

- The goalkeeper sprints down the slalom course through the poles.
- He does a side gallop down the course while keeping his face pointing always in the same direction.
- This time, as he runs through, in between the pairs of poles he twists his body round completely.
- He dribbles the ball through the slalom course.

- He runs across the poles, lifting the ball in the air a little each time he goes over a pole.
- He runs round the course bouncing the ball with the hand.
- He runs across the poles throwing the ball up and catching it. At the end of the course, the trainer throws another ball towards him, which he has to jump up and hit with his ball.

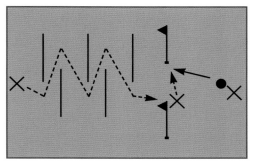

- The goalkeeper runs through the slalom course and positions himself in the goal mouth, that has been erected at the end, ready to save a surprise shot delivered at him in goal by the trainer.

Game play

- The trainer shoots 10 balls at goal. Beforehand, the trainer and the goalkeeper guess how many goals he will score and how many the goalkeeper will save. Whose guess was the most accurate?
- The trainer throws balls at the goalkeeper in all sorts of ways.
- The trainer throws bouncers at the goal. Each time he calls out to which side he is aiming. He is allowed to trick the goalkeeper.

12-14 YEARS

Exercise 2 – INDIVIDUAL TRAINING

Aims for the goalkeeper

- Diving sideways and catching medium height balls.
- Improvement in creating positional play.
- Long shots at goal.
- 1:1 situations.

Aims for the striker

- One-on-one with the goalkeeper, clever dribbling and scoring a goal.

Training partner

Attacking field player.

Getting in the mood/Warming up

Practice passing moves in pairs (goalkeeper and field player).

- Both do double passes to each other.
- In between the passes, the ball is held up in the air by juggling as long as possible.
- When it drops on the ground again, it has to be passed on.
- The couple carries out various stretching exercises that they are familiar with.
- The player in possession of the ball plays it on to his partner. He can use a feinting movement when he does so.
- The attacker kicks low balls at the goalkeeper, who makes a save and plays the ball back to the kicker.

Exercise main emphasis

- The goalkeeper does a forward roll and dives after the ball being kicked at him.
- The goalkeeper is lying on the ground on his stomach. He jumps up and dives after the ball being shot in by the attacker.

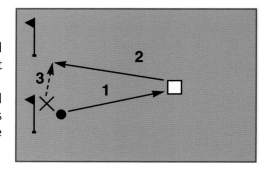

- The goalkeeper positions himself on the line in the goal mouth. The attacker shoots a placed ball at medium height, which the goalkeeper dives after. The striker may use feinting movements.
- With legs apart and with his back to the attacker, the goalkeeper stands in goal with the ball. He throws the ball through his legs to his partner, turns round quickly and dives after the shot coming in.

Game play

The goalkeeper and the attacker play against each other with two goal mouths, which are positioned about 25m apart.

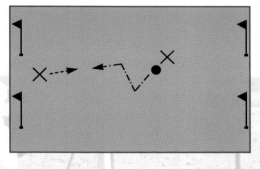

- The striker dribbles towards the goal and tries to get round the goalkeeper in a 1:1 situation. He may only score a goal from a close in position. In turn, the goalkeeper can punt any balls he saves straight into the opposing goal. Which of them is the most successful?
- The attacker shoots place shots at goal from 15m. The goalkeeper may kick any ball he saves with a low, long flat kick into the opposite goal.
- The attacker has to try to score a goal after dribbling and shooting from a distance. However, if the goalkeeper saves the ball, he may dribble it forward to score in the opposite goal. The attacker can try to save the goal, but without using his hands.

Exercise 3 INDIVIDUAL TRAINING

Aims

- Improvement of the speed of reaction.
- Firming up basic techniques.
- Getting used to the ball.

Training partner

A second goalkeeper/Co-trainer

Getting in the mood/Warming up

Both players have a ball each.

- They run and hop around with the ball, dribbling and bouncing it. When they pass by each other, they swap balls by bouncing them to each other.
- They keep changing balls by throwing them to each other. This is all done on the move.
- Playing copycat, the partner has to follow all the movements the goalkeeper does with his ball.
- Alternatively, instead of copying, the player following has to do a completely different movement to the one presented.
- They run alongside each other, dribbling the ball. Suddenly, 'A' throws his ball up in the air and 'B' has to catch it. Before this, however, 'B' has to throw his ball up in the air also, so that 'A' has to catch it.

Exercise main emphasis

- The goalkeeper is in goal. His partner kicks a football (or rugby ball) at goal.
- The partner throws the football at goal so that it bounces.
- The thrower has two balls, which he throws at goal in rapid succession and in different ways (high-low, right-left). The goalkeeper has to save them going in.

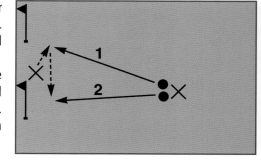

⚽ The goalkeeper kneels down on the goal line. His partner, with two balls, throws a high ball so that he has to stand up quickly to save the ball. The second ball then comes in straight away as a low ball so that he has to save it by doing a dive.

Game play

⚽ In a game 1:1 against two small goal mouths, both goalkeepers play as field players.

⚽ Two goal mouths are positioned 8-10m apart opposite each other. Both goalkeepers throw the ball at the other's goal.

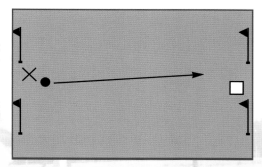

⚽ As before, but now the goal mouths are 10m apart. This time, placed kicks are shot at goal.

⚽ Goalkeeper 'A' throws his ball at his opponent, who tries to volley it into his opposing goal and score.

12-14 YEARS

Exercise 4 INDIVIDUAL TRAINING

Aims

- Improvement of ball control
- Improvement of the basic skills while being stretched to the limits.

Training partner

Trainer/Co-trainer

Getting in the mood/Warming up

The warm-up program is done with individual skills and with a ball.

- The goalkeeper dribbles the ball. Every now and again he pushes the ball a little forward, sprints after it and dives after it.
- On the trot, he bounces the ball with the right and the left hand. As he does this, he stops and dribbles the ball going down into a squatting position and back up again.
- He throws the ball up into the air backwards through his spread legs and then does a quick turn round and catches it.
- The goalkeeper does a few stretching exercises that he needs.
- While running along, he throws the ball up in the air with his right hand and catches it in his left hand.
- While running along with the ball at his feet, he kicks it up and catches it.

Exercise main emphasis

The goalkeeper is in goal while the trainer arranges 8 balls about 12m in front of the goal. The balls will be shot at goal in rapid succession, but in a way that the goalkeeper has a chance to deal with them.

- The goalkeeper squats down and in this position deflects the balls shot at him.
- The goalkeeper stands with knees bent (as if sitting on a seat) facing the trainer and deflects all the shots made at him.
- This time the goalkeeper defends the goal against the goal shots while lying on his stomach. The trainer must remember that the goalkeeper's radius of action is very limited while lying in this position.
- The trainer throws the balls at goal in quick succession, but changes the direction and height of each throw. The goalkeeper has to save the balls and quickly get back into his guard position.

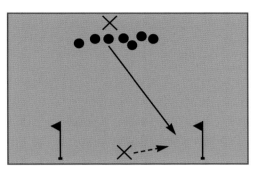
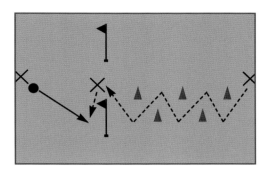

⚽ The goalkeeper runs forward zigzagging through a line of poles. He has to touch each pole with his hands and get himself quickly into position in goal before the trainer shoots at goal.

Game play

⚽ Play is in a game 5:5 against two small goal mouths without goalkeepers. The goalkeepers play as field players.

⚽ In a game between two teams of six players, the goalkeeper has to execute two very different tasks. He has to function as the goalkeeper for his team, but at the same time he is the only player on his team who may score a goal. Therefore, all the field players have to attack in a way so that the goalkeeper can score.

12-14 YEARS

Exercise 5 INDIVIDUAL TRAINING

Aims for the goalkeeper

- ⚽ Strengthening the offensive qualities.
- ⚽ Improvement of the defensive skills.

Aims for the field players

- ⚽ Work at goal scoring chances from various game situations.

Training partner

Attacking field players

Getting in the mood/Warming up

In pairs, they begin with varied passing situations.
- ⚽ By doing a skillful pass, the ball has to be in the air for as long as possible.
- ⚽ The pairs head the ball to one another.
- ⚽ The goalkeeper throws the ball high up to the attacker, who heads the ball back so that the goalkeeper has to take one or two steps before he can catch it.
- ⚽ The attacker kicks or throws the ball as fast as possible in the direction of the goalkeeper so that he is always on the move and has to strain for the ball.
- ⚽ By using either a throw out, a clearing kick or a place kick, the goalkeeper plays the ball at an attacker, who has to bring the ball under control as quickly as possible.

Exercise main emphasis

- ⚽ The goalkeeper is standing on his goal line. The attacker passes the ball to the goalkeeper from a point about 15m away. The goalkeeper kicks the ball back to the incoming trotting attacker who ends the exercise by shooting at goal.
- ⚽ From 15m out, the attacker kicks the ball to one side of the goal. The goalkeeper chases the ball and returns it to the attacker, who in turn dribbles the ball towards the goal to create a 1:1 situation.
- ⚽ The attacker shoots at goal, which the goalkeeper has to save. If the ball is returned to the attacker, he has a second chance at scoring a goal.

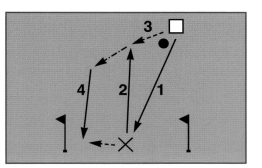

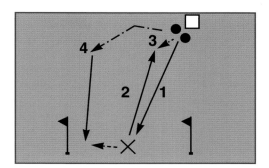

⚽ The attacker, standing at the edge of the 16m zone, has two balls. He kicks the first ball at the goalkeeper, who returns it so that a shot at goal comes in, and which the goalkeeper also has to save. Straight after this the attacker dribbles the second ball towards the goal and tries to play round the goalkeeper.

Game play

⚽ A game is played with 3 against 3, small goal mouths and without goalkeepers, who also play as field players. However, a goal can only be scored when each of the three on the team has touched the ball.

⚽ A game is played with 4 against 4, small goal mouths and no goalkeepers. A player can only score a goal for his team if he has not yet been successful. Which team is the first, where all four players have scored a goal?

Exercise 6 TEAM TRAINING

Aims for the goalkeeper

- Firming up the basic techniques.
- Organization of the defense.
- Schooling of tactics.

Aims for the field players

- Improvement of goal shooting techniques.
- Firming up team play.

Getting in the mood/Warming up

About fifteen balls are distributed around in an area 20m x 20m.

- All the players and the goalkeeper run around the area crisscrossing it and touching each ball alternately with the right and the left hand.
- Lying on the back, the ball is squeezed between the feet and lifted up.
- Each player is lying on the stomach and lifts a ball up with the hands three times and holds it up each time for 10 seconds. During this exercise, avoid incorrect breathing.
- The players are running around. The ball is lifted up and thrown up high in the air and caught again on the jump.
- At this point, several stretching exercises are programmed in.
- Dribble the ball to the next ball and leave it at that spot while taking on the ball that was lying there and dribbling it.

Exercise main emphasis

The goalkeeper is in goal and the field players practice goal shooting.

- The players dribble straight towards the goal and shoot from about 15m out.
- The players dribble the ball, coming in diagonally at the goal from the right or the left and end the run with a goal shot.
- Two players pass the ball between them as they run towards the goal. As they reach the 16m zone, the player with the ball ends up the run by shooting at goal.
- Pairs are formed. Partner 'A' stands on the center line with legs spread. 'B' passes the ball through 'A's' spread legs. Both sprint after the ball to get it. The winner shoots at goal.

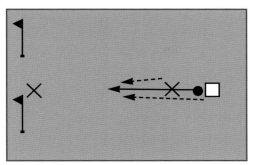

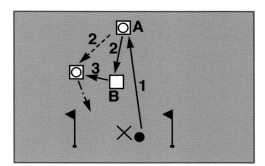

⚽ Partner 'A' is standing on the center line with 'B' around the edge of the 16m zone. The goalkeeper throws the ball out to 'A', who runs towards goal and passes it to 'B'. He returns it on the volley to 'A' who then engages the goalkeeper in a 1:1 situation.

Game play

A goalkeeper and five play against five, also with a goalkeeper.

⚽ When his own team is in possession of the ball, the goalkeeper plays as an additional field player. Any goals he scores count as three points.

⚽ While Team 'A' can only score goals with low shots, Team 'B' must score with medium height and high balls. In the second half, this form is reversed.

12-14 YEARS

Exercise 7 TEAM TRAINING

Aims for the goalkeeper

- Catching flanking balls.
- Improvement of positional play.
- Organization of the defense.

Aims for the field players

- Perfection of shooting techniques.
- Improvement of team play.

Getting in the mood/Warming up

The goalkeeper and the field players warm up together using games and exercises. This is done in one half of the pitch. A goalkeeper is positioned on each of the back lines.

- The aim, in a game of 6 against 6, is to kick the ball high so that the goalkeeper can catch it. The opposing team has to try to prevent these accurate passes happening.
- Each ball that is caught earns the team one point.
- The trainer whistles a stop to play several times. The ball is left lying on the ground and all players do some stretching exercises. Play is resumed when the trainer blows his whistle again.

Exercise main emphasis

- In the penalty area, two teams of the same strength play against each other at goal. The game is started, and similarly after each goal is scored, by the trainer delivering a flanking cross from the right or the left. They then challenge each other to score. If a player commits a foul, the person fouled is awarded a "penalty" shot. Only he can run towards the goal and take a shot. As soon as the goalie touches the ball, the chance is over.
- Four play against four with a single goal and a goalkeeper. Play starts when a neutral player kicks in a flanking cross at goal. These shots can be cleared in different ways. The goalkeeper can catch them, punch them away – they can also be headed or kicked into goal by a field player. Either one of the teams can also pass the ball amongst themselves and score a goal.

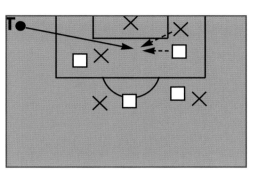

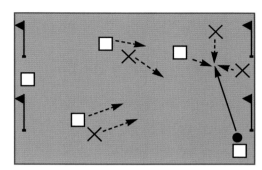

Game play

- Two teams play with two goal mouths, each with a goalkeeper. This time all the attacking play has to come in down the wing and end up with a flanking cross in front of goal. Goals only count when they follow a flanking cross.

- Two teams of the same strength play against each other with two goal mouths. Standard situations (corners, free kicks) play a special role in this exercise. Goals scored by attackers this way count double, irrespective of whether they are directly scored or come after combined play. Each goal saved by the defending team, however, also counts as double points.

Exercise 8 TEAM TRAINING

Aims for the goalkeeper

- Schooling of tactics.
- Improvement of defensive qualities.
- Improvement of positional play.

Aims for the field players

- Improvement of ball control.
- Strengthening tackling skills.
- Schooling of goal shooting.

Getting in the mood/Warming up

The warm-up is made livelier by using catching games.
- Less two catchers, all the other players plus the goalkeeper dribble the ball around in specified area (penalty box, center circle). The two catchers try to grab the ball as a goalkeeper would (diving for the ball, using the feet etc.). The player who loses the ball now has to bounce the ball around.
- The goalkeepers play as ball catchers. They have exactly 60 seconds to catch all the balls. Who manages to catch most?
- When a catcher has managed to get three balls off his colleagues, roles are changed over with the last person who had the ball.
- In pairs, the ball is passed between them. The two catchers try to break up the passing game and grab the ball.

Exercise main emphasis

- About 15m in front of a goal mouth, a larger area is marked out with poles. The players, who have been given a number by the trainer beforehand, dribble a ball freely around this area. The trainer now calls out a number, and that person immediately sets off towards goal and shoots at goal once he has left the marked-off area. The goalkeeper is named the winner if he can save at least 10 balls of the twenty shot at him.
- Using the same form of game, beforehand, the trainer decides the sequence of shooters, so that they can shoot at goal in quick succession.

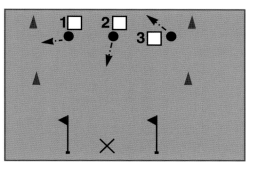 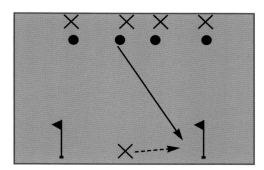

⚽ This time, each player is told beforehand where he has to place his shot (upper right, medium height left etc.). In this way, the goalkeeper always has to orient himself quickly and frequently.

⚽ The players lay their balls down along the 16m line. The trainer now calls out the name of the player, who then shoots at goal from this placed shot in different ways. Who manages to score the best goal?

Game play

In conclusion of the session, a little tournament is played 3:3. The goal mouth should be a medium width (5m wide).

⚽ In the first game, the goalkeeper plays as a field player.

⚽ In the second game, only the goalkeepers may score, but may not intervene to save others.

⚽ In the third game, the goalkeepers may only guard their own goal, and are not allowed to leave it to take part in the attack.

Question:

Which form of game was the greatest fun and which game takes the most fitness to do?

12-14 YEARS

Exercise 9 TEAM TRAINING

Aims for the goalkeeper

⚽ Improvement of offensive qualities.
⚽ Catching flanking crosses and high balls.

Aims for the field players

⚽ Improvement of ball handling techniques.
⚽ Close dribbling skills.
⚽ Delivering accurate flanking crosses.

Getting in the mood/Warming up

One half of the pitch is divided again into two halves. In the center of each of these smaller halves, a square 7m x 7m is marked off using poles. A goalkeeper is positioned in each of the squares. The players of the one team take up positions against the opposing goalkeeper in the playing area surrounding each of the squares. They pass the ball amongst themselves and have to pass it to their own goalkeeper in the other playing half. Each time the pass is successful they gain a point.

⚽ Using the same game situation as above, two balls are used.
⚽ The ball may be played with the hands and not the feet.

Exercise main emphasis

From either wing position, a flanking cross kick is played in towards goal alternately from the left and the right. Four attackers are waiting in the penalty area, and they are trying to score a goal. The goalkeeper has to save these goals.

⚽ Now, two defenders can help the goalkeeper in his efforts.
⚽ Three defenders are now covering the four attackers, and they try to stop a shot being taken.
⚽ The four attackers are now opposed by four defenders, who in turn, however, only cover the area. Beforehand, the trainer will specify the area in which the defenders can play.

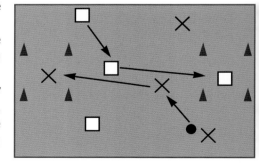

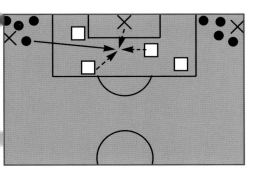
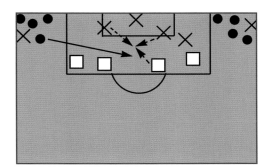

The flanking shots should be kicked in as hard and as low as possible from near to the sideline. They may also be kicked in behind the backs of the defenders. The attackers have to move about so that they are always possibly in unmarked positions.

Game play

The game is for 5 against 5 against two goals each with a goalkeeper. While the team in possession of the ball may use all of its players, the team that doesn't have the ball has to drop out two players, but these can take part again once their team regains possession of the ball. This way, the goalkeeper is kept very busy saving goals.

In the game above, if a goal is scored from a high flanking shot, it counts double points. If a goal is scored directly following a low flanking shot, then it counts even more – three times the points.

12-14 YEARS

Exercise 10 TEAM TRAINING

Aims for the goalkeeper

- Defense against long shots.
- Catching flanking crosses.
- Improvement of positional play.
- Control of the penalty area.

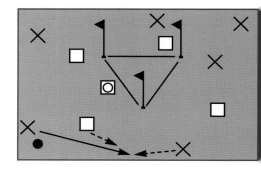

Aims for the field players

- Delivering accurate flanking kicks.
- Taking the ball cleanly.
- Volley shots.

Getting in the mood/Warming up

A triangular goal is marked off in the center of the playing area using poles. Six attackers play round the goal against four defenders and a goalkeeper. The goalkeeper has to keep changing his position according to which angle the play is developing, because a goal can be scored from all three goal sides. The players may not run through a 'goal mouth' to take a shortcut. The game continues even after a goal has been scored in order to keep exercising the player's fitness.

However, it makes sense to change round roles during the game. Time-outs can be planned, during which some stretching exercises can be done. Because there is a need to keep on coordinating between players, this costs a lot of concentration, especially when the players are working flat out.

- Players 'A' and 'B' kick flanking shots into the goal, and these should be played on by 'C', 'D' or 'E' to score a goal. Players 'F' and 'G' are taking a break. The goalkeeper has two possibilities. He can catch or deflect the flanker or wait for a direct shot or a header at goal.
- Players 'C' and 'D' kick flanking shots into the goal, and these should be played on by 'E', 'F' or 'G' to score a goal, while Players 'A' and 'B' try to stop them doing so.
- The goalkeeper throws the ball as high as possible. Players 'G','A' and 'B' try to kick the ball into goal as it drops, while players 'C' and 'D' try to stop them. Players 'E' or 'F' kick each ball that is saved back as a long shot at goal.

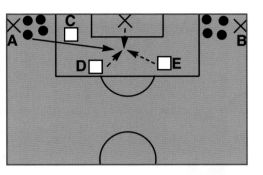

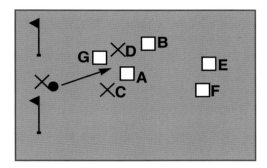

Game play

- With teams of 4:4, with two goals, a game of handball is played. However a goal can only be scored by heading after receiving it as a pass by another player. This means that the throw pass has to be done accurately. If the 'ref' whistles a foul, the "free kick", permissible only in the form of header, is taken from in front of the goal.
- In a soccer game with teams of four, this time the goalkeeper has to initiate rapid attacks. When he catches the ball, he has to throw it or kick it clear directly to the forward striker on his own team, so that he can try to score a goal on his own. In this game it is not the number of goals scored that count, but the number of goal chances coordinated.

12-14 YEARS

Eye on the ball!

14-18

15 TEN TRAINING SESSIONS FOR JUNIORS (AGED 14-18 YEARS)

Once again, as a summary, here are a few reminders about what aspects to think about for this phase for Juniors aged 14-18 years. `

- Basic goalkeeping techniques, learned so far in rough form, now have to be perfected and made automatic.

- The goalkeeper's playing ability must now be improved, especially regarding the improvement of his offensive play, so that he can use the ball as well as a field player.

- Once again, the coordination side of the development of a goalkeeper plays an important role.

- The goalkeeper now has to continue to increase his ability to organize the defenders in front of him and to be able to direct them what to do.

- His ability to control the penalty area will increase as he becomes challenged more and more.

- Power training, above all his jumping ability and speed, will improve his physical condition.

- In order to minimize the danger of injuries and so that the highest degree of preparedness is reached at the beginning of the game, stretching exercises must become an essential part of the warm-up.

- Development of the personality plays an important role, especially for goalkeepers. By being made responsible and accepting more responsibility, clear progress can be made in the development of this sphere.

YEARS

Exercise 1 INDIVIDUAL TRAINING

Aims

- Schooling of the speed of reaction.
- Improvement of coordination.

Training partner

- A second goalkeeper.

Getting in the mood/Warming up

- Both partners trot around doing arm circling and hopping exercises. The first goalkeeper carries out the exercise and his partner joins in the rhythm.
- The second goalkeeper throws the ball high up in the air while trotting round. The first goalkeeper jumps up towards it as high as possible, catches it and covers the ball against a tackle from his colleague.
- The two goalkeepers throw the ball to each other over a short distance.
- The goalkeepers toss the ball high to each other.
- The ball is thrown so that it bounces about 1m in front of the goalkeeper.
- Which goalkeeper can beat his colleague by dribbling the ball through his legs?

Exercise main emphasis

- The goalkeeper is kneeling down. His partner is standing a few meters behind him and throws the ball to the right or left past the goalkeeper. As soon as he 'senses' the ball coming he tries to deflect the ball in flight, reacting to it with his hands.
- The two goalkeepers are standing 2m opposite each other. Goalkeeper 'A' has a ball in each hand. Suddenly he lets either one of the balls drop and his partner has to dive after it before it touches the ground. As soon as the catcher loses his concentration, they swap over roles.
- One of the goalkeepers is standing in goal. The other one lines up about 8 balls next to each other, roughly 5m away from and in front of the goal. He now shoots the balls in rapid succession at the goal using different methods of kicking. The defending goalkeeper has to react to these as quickly as possible.
- The goalkeeper is standing in goal. His colleague kicks the ball up in the air in front of the goal mouth. The goalkeeper has to catch the ball, but is tackled by the kicker fairly as he does so.

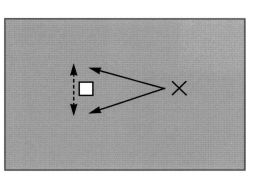

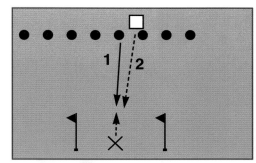

Game play

Two goal mouths are erected about 15m opposite each other and a goalkeeper is standing in each. Each goalkeeper now has to score as many goals as possible against his opponent. Each time he has to change the type of scoring the goal – for example, goals can be scored by:

- Winning a 1:1 situation.
- Volleying in a goalkeeper's clearing throw.
- Using a drop kick.
- Using a spot kick.

14-18 YEARS

Exercise 2 INDIVIDUAL TRAINING

Aims

- Strengthening the coordination ability.
- Improvement of the basic techniques.
- Getting used to the ball.

Training partner

A second goalkeeper.

Getting in the mood/Warming up

- Alternately, do forward and rearward press-ups over the ball lying on the ground.
- Lying on the stomach, the ball is pressed between the knees and lifted up a little.
- The ball is squeezed between the knees. They now do a forward roll so that the arms and the knees don't touch the ground.
- The goalkeeper lies down on his back and angles his legs. In this position, he throws the ball up in the air a little and catches it again.
- Now, dribbling is practiced, mainly by using the weaker foot.
- Stretching exercises are now carried out.
- Dribbling is done by using the knees or the elbows.

Exercise main emphasis

To improve techniques, four stations are used, where;

Station 1:   The goalkeeper has to dive after 10 balls, thrown at him by the second goalkeeper.

Station 2:   The goalkeeper has to save 10 shots at goal delivered by his colleague.

Station 3:   The one goalkeeper kicks 10 flanking crosses at goal and the other goalkeeper has to try to catch them at their highest point.

Station 4:   The goalkeeper saves 10 close shots at goal.

A run through the stations means that both of them get to do the exercise at each station so that their performance can be compared. It's important, however, that both goalies play fair with each other when they do the shooting.

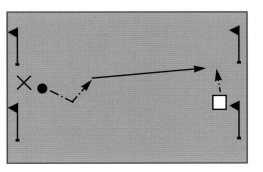 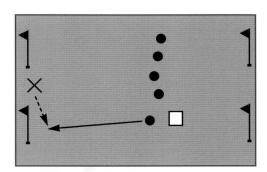

Game play

Play is done on one half of the pitch. A goal mouth is erected on each of the side ends of the pitch and the goalkeepers are positioned in these facing each other.

- The one goalkeeper dribbles the ball from his goal to the other and tries to score a goal against his opponent. If his colleague touches the ball with any part of his body, the attack is counted as over and the other goalie starts to do a dribbling attack.
- Each goalkeeper chooses five spots on the pitch, from where he believes he can score a goal. The spots have to be at least 12m from the goal.
- Whenever one goalkeeper is able to tackle the ball away from his partner, in turn, he can try to score a goal from a long shot.

14-18 YEARS

Exercise 3 INDIVIDUAL TRAINING

Aims

- Improvement of the basic techniques.
- Mastering standard situations.

Training partner

A second goalkeeper.

Getting in the mood/Warming up

- Both goalkeepers pass the ball between them on the move. The pass must drop properly in front of the other as he runs along so that he doesn't have to change his speed and step rhythm.
- Both of them throw the ball accurately to each other over longer distances while on the move.
- Stretching exercises are now carried out.
- The ball is thrown across to the partner in a way that he has to take a few quick steps to catch it.
- The ball is drop kicked to the partner, however, accurately so that the other doesn't have to move from his place.
- At this juncture, several gymnastic exercises are done to improve flexibility.
- The ball is thrown to the partner by a clearing throw. He checks the ball on his chest or stops it with his foot,

Exercise main emphasis

Two goal mouths are positioned 10-15m apart facing each other. A goalkeeper is positioned in each goal, and he has to try to score as many goals as possible in his opponent's goal. All the exercises are carried out against both goals.

- The ball is spot-kicked from the one goal 10 times at the opponent's goal.
- 10 balls are shot at the opponent's goal in the form of kick outs from the 10m point.
- From a distance of about 7m, the ball is thrown at the opponent's goal 10 times.
- From a distance of 4-5m the ball is thrown up high and headed 10 times at the goal.
- Each goalkeeper delivers 10 different kind of shots or throws at his opponent's goal as he sees fit.

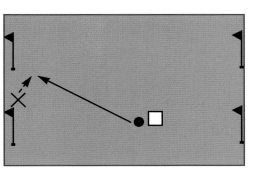

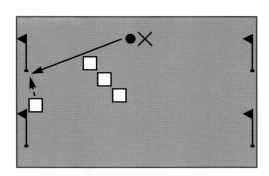

Game play

The goalkeepers play a game with the whole team. In the game, goals can only be scored from standard situations. This means using free kicks, corners and penalty shots. The trainer, acting as referee, has to be a bit generous in how the situations occur.

The main task of the goalkeeper is to position his defenders in each situation, placing a suitable wall if needed.

The task, for the team in possession of the ball, is to always try out using new variations (direct shots over the wall at goal, passing the ball to a teammate etc.). The attackers have to learn how best to disrupt the defense.

4-18 YEARS

Exercise 4 INDIVIDUAL TRAINING

Aims for the goalkeeper

- ⚽ Schooling the ability to react.
- ⚽ Defense against shots resulting from standard situations.

Aims for the striker

- ⚽ Scoring a goal in 1:1 situations.
- ⚽ Playing round the goalkeeper.

Training partner

Attacking players/offensive field players.

Getting in the mood/Warming up

- ⚽ The striker and the goalkeeper pass the ball to each other trotting along.
- ⚽ The attacker kicks in high balls, which the goalkeeper has to catch.
- ⚽ In a stretching session, the striker and the goalkeeper show each other exercises that are important for their warm-up. They then do the same exercise together.
- ⚽ Alternately, the goalkeeper and the attacker kick the ball forward from the same point and both of them then sprint after it. The goalkeeper may dive for the ball, while the striker is only allowed to touch the ball with his foot. Who reaches the ball first?
- ⚽ The attacker has to keep possession of the ball for as long as possible, protecting the ball with his body, while the goalkeeper is always trying to get hold of the ball.

Exercise main emphasis

- ⚽ The attacker dribbles the ball at goal and has to shoot the ball low before he reaches the 5m area.
- ⚽ The attacker dribbles the ball towards the goal. The goalkeeper tries to flatten the attack angle by running out towards the attacker. The attacker now has to outplay or play round the goalkeeper before he may shoot at goal.
- ⚽ The attacker, who is dribbling the ball towards the goal, has to start from the side line of the 5m zone. Once he is in the 5m zone he may shoot at goal.
- ⚽ The attacker has to stop the ball dead after it has been thrown out to him by the

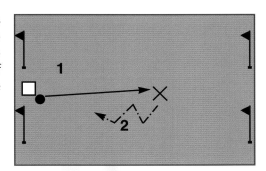

goalkeeper. Then the striker starts his lone run towards goal. Here he has to outplay the goalkeeper and shoot into an empty goal, thus gaining a point. If the goalkeeper manages to touch the ball, he gains one point.

Game play

- Play is 5:5 with a goalkeeper on each team in a shortened pitch. Goals may only be scored from individual lone attacks, thus these have to be started as fast as possible by their own goalkeeper using accurate throw outs or kick outs to create a surprise move. If the attacker can also outplay the goalkeeper and score, then he gets double points.
- Equal teams play against each other, but using particular rules. Each goal scored earns one point. A goal scored after an individual lone run earns two points. If the attacker manages to kick the ball through the goalkeeper's legs and score, this earns three points.

14-18 YEARS

Exercise 5 INDIVIDUAL TRAINING

Aims

- Improvement of jumping strength.
- Strengthening of agility.
- Firming up coordination.

Training partner

Trainer/Co-trainer

Getting in the mood/Warming up

- The goalkeeper runs around bouncing the ball, lets it drop and stops it with his stronger or weaker foot, dribbles along with that foot, lifts it up into his hand and continues bouncing the ball.
- Running around, the goalkeeper does arm circling, hopping, turning the body round, forward rolls, flying dives and jumps with one leg and both legs.
- Now he does stretching exercises.
- The goalkeeper punts the ball up high and catches it again. As he does this he jumps up as high as possible towards the ball.
- The goalkeeper bounces the ball along against an imaginary opponent.
- The goalkeeper kicks the ball into the center circle and immediately sprints after it. He has to gather the ball up safely before it stops rolling.

Exercise main emphasis

- The trainer passes the ball at the goalkeeper over short distances and he has to save them with his feet.
- From a short distance, the trainer kicks the ball at goal, which the goalkeeper should deflect (i.e., not catch).
- The goalkeeper is lying on his back. From this position he throws the ball up high, stands up quickly and tries to catch the ball on the jump.

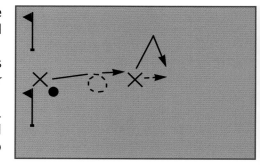

- The goalkeeper is holding the ball firmly in both hands, does a forward roll, throws the ball forwards a little and tries to gather it up by diving after it.
- The goalkeeper squeezes the ball firmly between his feet, jumps up and whips the ball up and tries to catch it with both hands.
- The trainer is continually throwing high balls at the goalkeeper, which he has to catch at their highest point in the air and pass back to the trainer.
- The trainer bounces the ball hard onto the ground and the goalkeeper has to catch it. The trainer then squats on the ground and the goalkeeper has to jump over him. Finally, the trainer extends one of his arms out sideways and the goalkeeper has to do a jumping forward roll over it. The trainer changes the various exercises round and invents a few more.

Note:

During all the jumping exercises attention must be paid that the goalkeeper is not overstrained. Don't forget to incorporate working time-outs (loosening exercises, trotting)!

Game play

- After an intensive session of jumping training, it is quite sensible to get the goalkeeper to play as a field player and devote his time to improving his playing qualities.
- A tournament is played with teams of 3:3. Each team plays against all the others for 5-7 minutes.

14-18 YEARS

Exercise 6 TEAM TRAINING

Aims for the goalkeeper

- ⚽ Saving long shots.
- ⚽ Catching flanking shots.
- ⚽ Improvement of throwing clearances.

Aims for the field players

- ⚽ Practicing spot kicks from a distance.
- ⚽ Improving ball control.
- ⚽ Changing speed and direction.

Getting in the mood/Warming up

The goalkeepers do their warming up with the team.

- ⚽ The whole team is divided into groups of four. In a specified area, the groups of four pass the ball between themselves, and each man plays for himself. Field players pass the ball using their feet, while goalkeepers pick the ball up in their hands and throw it to their teammates.
- ⚽ In a game with the goalkeeper against three players, he has to challenge the others for the ball. To start with, the players can stop the ball, then, later, they have to pass it on straight away.
- ⚽ In a game with the goalkeeper against three, the goalkeeper has to tackle the ball away from the others with his feet. Players receiving the ball have to pass it on straight away.
- ⚽ The ball has to be kept up in the air between three players standing in a triangle. First of all, the goalkeeper can gain the ball using his hands, but then later, play it on only with his head.

Exercise main emphasis

- ⚽ A goalkeeper is in each of two goal mouths facing each other. Goalkeeper 'A' throws the ball to the players, who now dribble towards Goal 'B' and, from a distance of about 15-20m, shoot at goal. Goalkeeper 'B' tries to catch the ball or stop it, and throws it to one of his own teammates, who dribbles off straight away towards Goal 'A'.

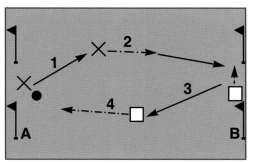

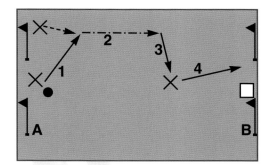

- Goalkeeper 'A' throws the ball to a wing player, who runs with it towards Goal 'B' down the flank. As he reaches the level of the goal, he crosses the ball from the flank in to the front of the goal. A teammate is standing there and has to score a goal from the flanking shot, which, of course, the goalkeeper has to save.
- Once again the ball is dribbled down the wing towards the opponent's goal. A teammate is running down the middle of the field parallel to him, and tries to score a goal. However, this time not only the goalkeeper will try to stop the goal, a defender is also there to support him.

Game play

- The players divide themselves up into two teams (e.g., defensive players together and offensive players together) and play on the full pitch. Each team needs to have a goalkeeper. The aim, of course, is to score goals! However, the rules are different. If the defenders score a goal, they earn two points. If the offensive players manage to stop a goal, they also get two points.
- Two teams, each with a goalkeeper, play against each other. However, because the aim is to score goals using long shots, the rules are as follows: A goal scored from up to 10m out earns one point. Scored from up to 20m out, the goal earns two points, with three points earned for goals scored from longer distances.

14-18 YEARS

Exercise 7 TEAM TRAINING

Aims for the goalkeeper
⚽ Catching high balls and flanking shots.
⚽ Throw out clearances direct to own players.

Aims for the field players
⚽ Delivering flanking crosses.
⚽ Scoring a goal from flanking shots and high balls using the foot or a header.

Getting in the mood/Warming up
Passing is practiced on the move in groups of three. The goalkeeper slips in as a field player.
⚽ Accurate passing to a teammate is practiced over short distances. The teammate has to take the ball on cleanly and pass it on.
⚽ Short distance passes are practiced, with the ball being passed on straight away.
⚽ The ball is kicked in as a long high ball so that the partner can receive the ball easily.
⚽ The ball is thrown as per a throw-in.
⚽ The third player is standing in between the two other players, who throw the ball or play it with the feet to each other. The man in the middle must avoid being hit by the ball.
⚽ The three players throw the ball to each other over longer distances. The goalkeeper doesn't try to catch the ball, but punches it out to a teammate.

Exercise main emphasis
All the players run along the left or right sidelines of the pitch and kick flanking shots accurately into the front of the goal. The trainer directs what is to happen, such as:
⚽ A flanking shot at the near or the far goalpost.
⚽ A flanking shot as close as possible to the goal.
⚽ A flanking shot that turns away from the goal.
⚽ A low flanking shot.

The goalkeeper is kept in the dark about which flanking shot is coming in, and has to adapt his position against all the possibilities. He has to try, as safely as possible, to either catch the ball, punch it out or deflect it. When punching the ball out back into play, he has to tip it up high and not at medium height. To make it more difficult for the goalkeeper, an attacker can be brought in, who tries to challenge the goalie in his attempts.

Game play

⚽ On one half of the pitch, 5 play against 5 with two goal mouths and two goalkeepers. On each side of the pitch there is 5m-wide 'out of bounds' zone, which can only be used by one wing player of each team at any one time. The player may not be tackled in this zone, therefore, he is able to place his flanking shot directly at the goal.

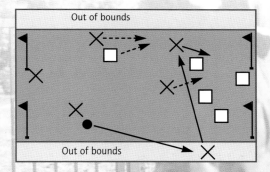

Out of bounds

Out of bounds

⚽ The goalkeeper has two possibilities for his action against a flanking shot, or against the follow up shot or header at goal. If he is able to catch the ball, he earns two points. If he saves a goal (by deflecting), he gets one point. On the other hand, when the attackers score, they only get one point.

⚽ In a game 5:5, any foul (or when balls go out) is followed by a corner kick. If the goalkeeper catches the ball, he gets three points. If he deflects the ball to the side or over the bar, he gets two points. If he punches it away, he gets one point. Any goal scored earns only one point.

14-18 YEARS

Exercise 8 TEAM TRAINING

Aims for the goalkeeper

- Safely saving difficult shots.
- Saving long shots.
- Improvement of field playing qualities.

Aims for the field players

- Improvement of ball control.
- Tactics in game situations.
- Covering the playing area.

Getting in the mood/Warming up

- All the players and the goalkeeper keep busy on the move.
- The goalkeeper demonstrates some tricks with the ball, which the other players copy.
- In a game of catch, the goalkeeper plays against the 10 other players, who have to pass the ball between them without moving from the spot. The goalkeeper, on the other hand, can use any opportunity he can think of to get the ball.
- In the second round of the same game, the players have to keep the ball up in the air. This time, on the other hand, the goalkeeper may only get possession of the ball by using his body, head or legs. He may not use his arms or hands.

Exercise main emphasis

Three equal strength teams are formed. Each time two teams play against each other, while the third team does some technique practice, using stations. Each team plays against the others for a period of 10 minutes. The goalkeepers are positioned in goal for the games.

With the goalkeeper in mind, both competing teams have to play as follows:
- As many long shots at goal have to be made.
- The ball has to be shot low at goal.
- As often as possible, the goalkeeper is made to face 1:1 situations.

The stations for practicing techniques are as follows:

Station 1: Dribbling the ball down a slalom course.

Station 2: Sprinting after a steep pass.

Station 3: Keeping the ball up in the air.

Station 4: Dribbling and changing direction frequently.

Station 5: Shots at a 1m-wide goal mouth from a distance of 12-15m.

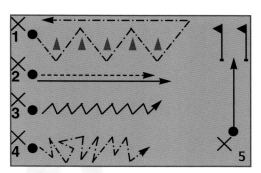

Game play

◉ Teams of seven plus a goalkeeper play against each other. Each team has four attackers and three defenders, and they may only carry out their main positional tasks in their area (i.e., attackers may only attack and defenders, defend). At the same time, the attackers are always in a majority situation. They have to use passes between themselves until they have outplayed all their opponents, and end up where a single attacker can move towards the goal on his own. Only goals scored in this manner count, once the player can cross the goal line together with the ball.

◉ Two teams of four play against a goalkeeper in one goal. Each time a player enters the penalty area he has to shoot at goal immediately. This way the goalkeeper will be faced with lots of goal shots.

14-18 YEARS

Exercise 9 TEAM TRAINING

Aims for the goalkeeper

- Organization of the defense.
- Quick changeovers on to the offensive.

Aims for the field players

- Improvement of passing play.
- Practicing counterattacks.

Getting in the mood/Warming up

The goalkeeper trains together with the field players.

- The field players are standing round the goalkeeper in a circle. Suddenly, they start running away from him and he has to throw the ball into their paths so that they can take on the ball without any problem.
- The goalkeeper drop kicks several balls onto the pitch one after the other. The players have to chase after them and bring them under control. From this point, where they end up with the ball, they have to play it back to the goalkeeper as accurately as possible.
- A stretching exercise period is now done, led by one of the goalkeepers.
- The attackers carry out free kicks from various different positions. When doing so, they think up new dodges and tricks. The goalkeeper sets his defenders according to where he thinks they can hinder play.

Exercise main emphasis

Play is against three goals. Besides the main goal mouth, guarded by a goalkeeper, two small goal mouths are erected on the center line using flags. These are not guarded by goalkeepers. Team 'A', consisting of the goalkeeper, all the defenders and some midfield players, has to defend the large goal mouth. Team 'B', consisting of attackers and offensive midfielders try to score goals in the big

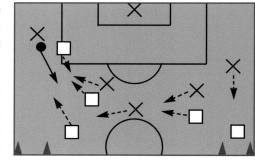

goal. At the same time, Team 'B' has to watch out that Team 'A', when in possession of the ball, is not able to start a rapid counter-attack towards the two smaller 'flag' goals. The following tasks can be done:

- The ball is exclusively kicked low and flat.
- The ball is passed on as straight away as possible.
- The ball may only be passed on after an opponent has been out-played following a dribbling movement.

Game play

Play is against two small goals without goalkeepers. They play as field players instead.

- Only goals scored by the goalkeeper count.
- The goalkeeper is used as a defender.
- Differently to the other field players, the goalkeeper may bounce the ball along. The opponents have to try and get the ball off him by using their feet, body or head.
- Although he belongs to one of the sides, if the goalkeeper gains possession of the ball, he may change sides. His teammates have to pay particular attention to when he might use this choice, and immediately switch on to this new situation.

14-18 YEARS

Exercise 10 TEAM TRAINING

Aims for the goalkeeper

- Improvement of the reaction to shots at goal from close in.
- Strengthening his field player qualities.

Aims for the field players

- Direct passing play.
- Goal shots from close in.

Getting in the mood/Warming up

Groups of four are formed, to include a goalkeeper, and they practice passing.

- Passing is practiced over short distances of a few meters. The ball is kept low.
- The passes are delivered hard. The ball has to be stopped first and then passed on.
- After a hard pass, the ball is directly passed on.
- The ball is thrown hard from a short distance and has to be caught or at least deflected.
- The ball is thrown and is deflected in its flight path, but still has to be caught safely.
- The players circle round, passing and throwing the ball to each other. The person with the ball can change direction of the circle whenever he wants to.

Exercise main emphasis

The whole training group can be divided up into three sections.

Section 1: Play is with 3:3 against two small goal mouths. Neither team may dribble the ball. It has to be passed on directly after received.

Section 2: Play is with 3:2 against a goal and goalkeeper. While the team in the majority do five attacks, the outnumbered team and the goalkeeper have the task of defending.

Section 3: This team practices the direct short passing game while constantly being on the move. Here, the ball may be kicked low or at medium height and should be at a sharp angle to the goal.

All the sections change over their exercise after a period of about 10 minutes.

Game play

- Play is done on the whole pitch. Each team, in its own half, is permitted to field only half its players plus 1. For example, if a team consists of 10 or 11 players, in the attack or in the defense, they may only field a maximum of six players. This ruling guarantees that each attack has more room to develop, and intensively challenges the defenders more.

- The game is played over the whole pitch. This time dribbling is allowed. The ball has to be passed on after it has been touched three times.

- The ball has to be passed on in a different way than received. For example, if a player receives a high ball, he must pass it on low or at medium height.

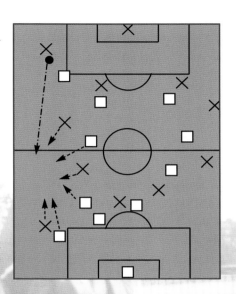

SE

16 TEN TRAINING SESSIONS FOR SENIORS

The content of training for Seniors shows a strong similarity to the exercises for the 14-18 year olds. As a reminder here are a few pointers:

- Yet again, the schooling of coordination is an important aspect in goalkeeper training.

- Perfecting the basic techniques, which a goalkeeper has to be able do automatically, is equally a part of the content. His ability to react well on the goal line is also just as decisive, as well as his eye to initiate game winning chances in front of the goal.

- His capability to control the penalty area will be constantly improved, thanks to the experience he has gained.

- In order to be able to put all his abilities into action optimally, schooling of speed and jumping ability, the strengthening of all of his muscles and his concentration must be practiced further.

- Of course, the playing ability of the goalkeeper must also be as equal as that of a field player if he wants to be good at his job.

- Not least of all, the development of the goalkeeper's personality plays an important role in the structure of his team. He has to be able to direct the defense and command a completely clear overview of the opportunities that any game situation may offer.

Exercise 1 INDIVIDUAL TRAINING

Aims for the goalkeeper

- ⚽ Tactics in a 1:1 situation.
- ⚽ Basic techniques in a 1: 1 situation.

Aims for the attacker

- ⚽ Scoring a goal in a 1:1 situation.
- ⚽ Ball control.

Training partner

Attacker – also Trainer/Co-trainer

Getting in the mood/Warming up

- ⚽ Goalkeeper and attacker stand in front of each other about 5-8m apart, but a little offset to each other. The attacker kicks the ball at a right angle at the goal. The goalkeeper has to take one or two steps to pick the ball up and then he rolls it out again to the attacker. He also has to take one or two steps in order to be able to take the ball on with his foot.

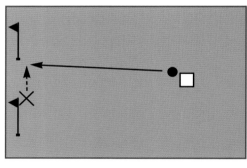

- ⚽ In the second round, the ball is kicked in at medium height.
- ⚽ Stretching exercises are then done.
- ⚽ This time the goalkeeper doesn't take steps to get to the ball, but dives after it.
- ⚽ A few gymnastics exercises round off the warm-up.

Main training emphasis

The attacker shoots the ball at goal from different positions. The goalkeeper has to catch the balls or save them.

- ⚽ The ball is kicked at goal from the penalty spot.

- The ball is place kicked at goal from the corner of the 16m area.
- The ball is place kicked at goal from various points around the 5m area. Above all, kicks from the sides of this area should be concentrated on.
- The ball is dribbled towards the goal and, at about 12m out from the goal, a shot is made.
- The attacker tries to dribble round the goalkeeper. This exercise is done both directly at the goalie as well as from the side.
- In a final game 1:1, using two small goal mouths, each goal scored by the goalie counts as double.

Game play

- Two groups of four play against each other with goalkeepers. The goalkeeper kicks the ball well up the field where the players challenge each other for the ball. The team in possession of the ball has to score a goal within 20 seconds of an attack started by their goalie (with the clearing kick). If this isn't managed the ball is returned to the goalkeeper and the opponents earn a point.

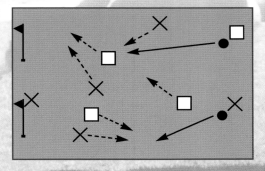

- Two groups of four play against each other at one goal mouth. But this time, there are two balls on the field. The players and the goalkeeper now have to concentrate on two games, as a goal can be scored with either ball.

SENIORS

Exercise 2 INDIVIDUAL TRAINING

Aims for the goalkeeper

- ⚽ Improvement of coordination.
- ⚽ Increasing the reaction senses.

Training partner

Trainer/Co-trainer

Getting in the mood/Warming up

The trainer practices passes to the goalkeeper.

- ⚽ The goalkeeper adopts a crouching stance. The trainer throws balls at him from the side, which the goalie has to catch or dive after.
- ⚽ The trainer kicks low balls at the goalkeeper, which the goalkeeper has to deflect or catch.
- ⚽ The goalkeeper is in the on guard position and the ball is played to him as a bouncer.
- ⚽ The trainer throws high balls at the goalkeeper, who has to catch them as safely as possible.
- ⚽ In between, a few stretching exercises are carried out or a time-out breather is taken by trotting around.

Main training emphasis

Tires are used as equipment for the schooling of coordination.

- ⚽ They run along through the tires as fast as possible.
- ⚽ They hop along through the tires.
- ⚽ They bounce a ball as they run through the course.
- ⚽ They run through the course dribbling a ball, which may not touch any of the tires.
- ⚽ When running through the tires, they throw a ball up and catch it again.
- ⚽ After this, the following tasks have to be done at the various stations:

Station 1: Running jumps through the tires.
Station 2: Sprinting in a slalom round through the line of tires.
Station 3: Placing a foot into a tire and jumping out of it again with increasing speed.
Station 4: Doing a squat in each tire and then diving after a ball thrown at them by the trainer.

Game play

⚽ The goalkeeper sprints down through the line of tires, then does a slalom round through the second group of tires and sprints into goal. Once he is there, the trainer shoots at goal.

⚽ The goalkeeper does a sprint and a slalom through the tires again, but this time carrying a ball, which he shoots at goal after he has done the slalom. He carries on to get back in goal, because the trainer is standing behind the goal, at which he shoots a ball.

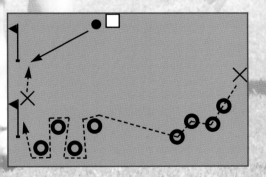
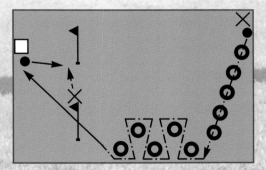

SENIORS

Exercise 3 INDIVIDUAL TRAINING

Aims

- Strengthening of the trunk muscles.
- Improvement of jumping strength.
- Observing play.
- Improvement of the reaction senses.

Training partner

Trainer/Co-trainer.

Getting in the mood/Warming up

The goalkeeper plays around busily with the ball.

- He throws the ball up high and catches it on a jump.
- The ball is bounced on the spot as the goalkeeper squats down.
- The goalkeeper is lying on his back and throws the ball up vertically. Then he sits up and catches the ball.
- He is lying on his stomach and is bouncing the ball. Continuing to bounce the ball, he turns his body over in a complete turn.
- Stretching exercises follow.
- Lying on his back, the goalkeeper throws the ball up high and smashes the dropping ball away using both feet, like when doing an overhead falling kick.
- Sitting propped up like a bench seat, the goalkeeper rolls the ball round on the ground between his feet and hands.
- Running around, the goalkeeper kicks the ball high up in the air and catches the dropping ball using a diving jump.

Main training emphasis

In a marked-off area, there are 8 medicine balls scattered about on the ground.

- The goalkeeper sprints from ball to ball, throws them up, catches them on a jump and lays them back down again.
- He sprints again from ball to ball, throws them up backwards through his spread legs, turns round and catches them again.

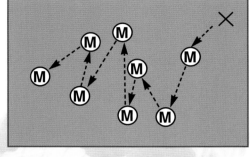

- Again, the goalkeeper sprints round all the balls and hops over each ball five times. After each hop, he does a forward roll before he runs on to the next ball.
- He sprints to each ball. Lying on the back, the ball is kicked up and before he catches the ball, he has to stand up quickly first.
- After sprinting to the ball, the goalkeeper lies down on his stomach and throws the ball at the next neighboring ball, stands up again and sprints to that ball where he carries out the same exercise again.

Game play

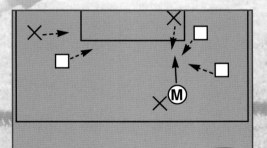

- With small teams such as 3:3 or 4:4, a game of "Pushball" is played in a specific area (the penalty area) where a medicine ball has to be pushed over a particular line. The goalkeeper plays as a field player.
- A game of "Roll-ball" is played between two teams of four where the ball has to be rolled along the ground using the hand. Also here, the ball has to be rolled over a particular line.

Note:

After each exercise, it is a good idea to take an active, recovery time-out where the goalkeeper does an exercise of balancing the ball.

SENIORS

Exercise 4 INDIVIDUAL TRAINING

Aims

- ⚽ Improvement of speed.
- ⚽ Strengthening the reaction senses.
- ⚽ Improvement of the coordination.

Training partner

A second goalkeeper.

Getting in the mood/Warming up

- ⚽ The couple warm up together by passing the ball to each other.
- ⚽ The two goalkeepers do a loose trot around passing the ball using their strong foot, but also occasionally using their weaker foot.
- ⚽ The passing moves take place over short distances of maximum 5m.
- ⚽ Passing is now done at distances of approximately 10m. The receiving goalkeeper gathers the ball on the move, drops it down on to his foot and passes it on to his partner again.
- ⚽ A few exercises are selected from the stretching program.
- ⚽ Passes are made using distant, lofting balls. The receiver has to try and catch the ball in the air.
- ⚽ Running along sideways, the two goalkeepers pass the ball to each other as per a throw-in.

Main training emphasis

A line of poles or tires is laid down. At the end is a goal mouth.

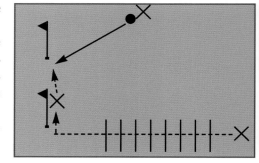

- ⚽ The goalkeeper sprints down the line of poles first of all and then rushes into the goal mouth, where he waits for a ball to be thrown at him. The second goalkeeper, who is standing on the other side of the goal, throws this in.

- A slalom is done down the line of poles. After sprinting to get in the goal mouth, a low shot is sent in at him by the other goalkeeper.
- The goalkeeper runs down the line of poles and first of all the other one throws a ball at him, followed up immediately by a further kick at goal.
- He runs down the line of poles again. After the last pole, a forward roll is done and a high ball is shot in at goal.

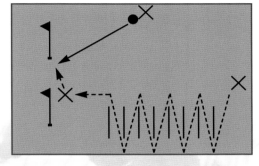

- The distance between the poles is increased so that the goalkeeper has to take two steps between each pole. As before, a ball is thrown or kicked at goal.
- The goalkeeper runs round the end of each pole and gets into the goal mouth to save a throw or a shot at goal by his colleague. This time, however, he can use a feinting movement.

Game play

- Two teams of three play against each other with two small goal mouths and no goalkeepers. They play as field players. Each player is nominated an opponent to mark whenever the other team is in possession of the ball. When his own team has the ball, he has to keep himself unmarked so he can receive a pass.
- In a game of slow motion soccer 3:3 against small goal mouths, all movements are done slowly. When the trainer gives a signal, normal play is resumed. When the trainer gives another signal, they go back to slow motion movements.

SENIORS

Exercise 5 INDIVIDUAL TRAINING

Aims for the goalkeeper

- Fitness improvement.
- Strengthening the coordination.

Aims for the attacker

- Improvement of speed.
- Using the ball.

Training partner

Attacker/Offensive field player.

Getting in the mood/Warming up

Both start off by running around loosely and passing the ball to each other.
- They pass the ball with their feet.
- The attacker kicks the ball low at the goalkeeper, who picks it up and rolls it back again.
- The attacker plays in a high ball, which the goalkeeper catches and throws back to the attacker. He kicks it high straight back at the goalkeeper. Thus both of the players are constantly on the move, as is the ball.
- A few exercises are done from the stretching program.
- The attacker kicks the ball high at the goalkeeper. He catches it and throws it into the attacker's path so that he has to sprint to get it.

Main training emphasis

1:1, play is against a small goal mouth and a large one. The goalkeeper defends the larger one as he normally would. The attacker has to guard the smaller one, but is not allowed to use his hands.
- The attacker has ten balls on the edge of the penalty area, which he shoots,

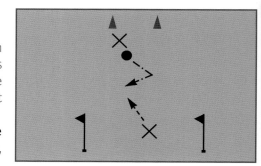

one after the other, at goal. The
goalkeeper tries to save or deflect as
many balls as he can.

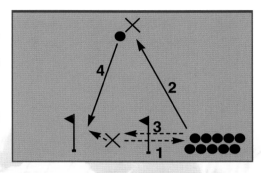

- Ten balls are positioned to one side of
the goal. The goalkeeper passes them,
one by one, to the attacker. After each
pass out, the goalkeeper has to get
back quickly into goal to stop that ball
being kicked in directly by the attacker
again.
- The attacker lines up ten balls in front of the goal about 12m away from it. He kicks
these as fast as possible at goal and in doing so takes no notice of where the
goalkeeper is. He only wins when he has managed to score at least six goals.
- The attacker deliberately tries to hit the crossbar or goal post. Because such balls are
difficult to judge, the goalkeeper must keep his wits about him.

Game play

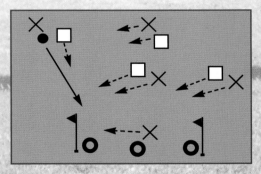

- Two equal strength teams play with
normal rules at a goal. However, three
tires are hanging up in the goal mouth
(in the middle and one at each side). If
a goal is scored, and it goes through
one of the tires, the goal is counted as
double. Of course, in front of the tires
is the goalkeeper who tries to stop the
attacker and save goals using any
means.
- The three tires can also be hung at different heights and in the event of a goal being
scored, count differently.

SENIORS

Exercise 6 TEAM TRAINING

Aims for the goalkeeper

- Improvement of the basic techniques under intense fitness conditions.
- Schooling the coordination.

Aims for the attacker

- Long shots from a spot kick.
- Improvement of passing moves.
- Tactical moves.

Getting in the mood/Warming up

A group of five carries out passing moves. In this, the goalkeeper, who plays with them, has special tasks. The players stand round in a square, while the goalkeeper is in the middle.

- The players pass the ball low to each other and pull the goalkeeper into these moves. These are done by first stopping the ball and then passing, and later they are passed directly on.
- Only the players pass the ball amongst themselves, while the goalkeeper tries to get the ball by running and diving for it.
- The ball is headed between the players, first of all including the goalkeeper, but later he has to try and catch the ball.
- The players keep the ball up in the air. Before passing the ball on like this, each player is allowed to touch the ball up to three times. The goalkeeper, on the other hand, has to try and get the ball off them.

Main training emphasis

- The goalkeeper takes up his position in goal. Each player dribbles his ball at goal and sends in a shot from a spot, which has been marked by the trainer beforehand.
- In rapid succession, all the players now dribble towards the goal and kick in a

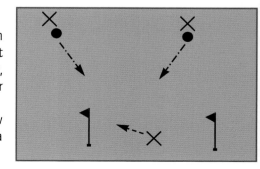

long shot so that the goalkeeper is heavily loaded, demanding a lot of concentration from him.

⚽ Two players, each with their own ball, dribble towards goal at the same time and shoot at goal at the same moment. The goalkeeper has to decide which ball he can best defend the goal against.

⚽ Once again, two players, each with their own ball, dribble at the same time towards the goal. One player comes in from the right and the other from the left. When they reach the goalkeeper, however, they have to outplay him. But the second player only gets a chance to outnumber him if the first is successful.

⚽ Four players run at goal from different directions, at intervals of four seconds. They try to beat the goalkeeper by delivering long shots at goal. Because of the short interval in time, the goalkeeper has continually to react quickly.

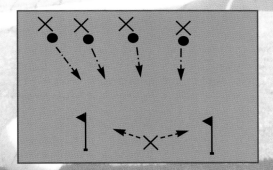

Game play

A game is played in three zones. The pitch is divided up into three. A goalkeeper is placed in each goal mouth. In each third, there are 4 attackers and two defenders. In the middle third, they play 5:5. Players may not leave their third of the pitch. On the boundary of the third, the ball has to be passed to another member of the same team.

⚽ The attackers are in the majority and therefore can shoot at goal more often.

⚽ The defenders are outnumbered and therefore their fitness comes into play.

⚽ The midfield is very busy with players. Because of this, a lot of tackles and challenging for possession of the ball takes place.

SENIORS

Exercise 7 TEAM TRAINING

Aims for the goalkeeper

- ⚽ Tactical measures.
- ⚽ Improvement of field player qualities.

Aims for the attacker

- ⚽ Improvement of team play.
- ⚽ Fitness training.

Getting in the mood/Warming up

Two teams are formed. Each team has a goalkeeper.

- ⚽ The teams pass the ball amongst themselves on the move.
- ⚽ When passing amongst the team, the ball may be touched only once.
- ⚽ All the team members form a circle. A further field player stands in the center of the circle, and his teammates keep on passing a ball to him. It is the goalkeeper's job to prevent this happening.
- ⚽ The whole team does some stretching exercises.
- ⚽ All the players stand in a circle. The goalkeeper is in the center of the circle. The person in possession of the ball dribbles this now to a teammate, who takes over the ball and he dribbles it on to another teammate. However, all the dribbling actions must go through the center of the circle where the goalkeeper is waiting to get the ball off them.

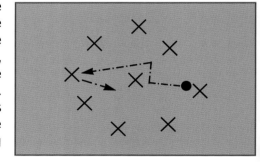

Main training emphasis

- ⚽ Play is with 5:5 against two small goal mouths (3-4m wide) and goalkeepers. The goalkeepers have to stop the ball with both hands.
- ⚽ In a game with 5:5 against two small goal mouths and goalkeepers, they may only stop the ball with one hand and either foot. Goal shots may only be made after a body feint has been done.

⚽ Under the same game conditions, the goalkeeper may only save the ball with his feet and his body. The use of the hands is strictly forbidden.

⚽ In a game with 5:5 against two small goal mouths and goalkeepers, they may do saves as normal this time. Additionally, the goalie may act as the only field player who may catch a high ball with the hands and score a goal by throwing it in.

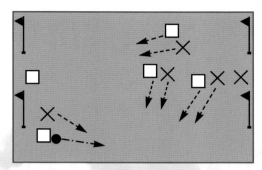

Game play

Play is against a goal guarded by a goalkeeper. On the pitch there are six attackers playing against four defenders. While the outnumbered team has only to keep the ball in possession as long as possible, the team with the majority has to score goals. Each time the team of six fails to score a goal from a shot, a point is awarded to the team of four.

⚽ In a similar game situation, each member of the team of six may only touch the ball twice in quick succession.

⚽ Same game – but this time the goalkeeper can be included in the passing and holding of the ball by the team of four.

SENIORS

Exercise 8 TEAM TRAINING

Aims for the goalkeeper

- ⚽ Improvement of field player qualities.
- ⚽ Managing back passes.
- ⚽ Strengthening the basic techniques.

Aims for the attacker

- ⚽ Ball control.
- ⚽ Improvement of the accuracy of long shots.

Getting in the mood/Warming up

- ⚽ Player 'A' dribbles the ball, changing his speed and direction regularly. Player 'B' follows on behind him. Then they change roles.
- ⚽ Player 'A' dribbles the ball and is followed by Player 'B'. Suddenly 'A' kicks an angled pass and both players sprint after the ball to gain possession of it.
- ⚽ Players 'A' and 'B' juggle the ball between them, keeping it up in the air.
- ⚽ At this juncture, they do stretching exercises.
- ⚽ Player 'A' dribbles the ball along, while Player 'B' tries to run him off the ball and get it.
- ⚽ Player 'A' dribbles the ball along at a steady speed and 'B' follows him. When the trainer gives a signal, 'A' tries to get away free from 'B'.

Main training emphasis

Two goals are erected about 40-50m away from each other.

- ⚽ One after the other, the players dribble the ball at Goal 'A' and send a back pass to the goalkeeper. They then run off into a free area where they receive a pass from the goalkeeper again. They then dribble towards Goal 'B' and deliver a long shot at goal. After a while, the other goalkeeper carries out the same exercise.

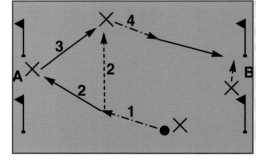

- One after the other, all the players run towards Goal 'A' and pass the ball back to the goalkeeper. They then run into a free area where they receive the ball back from the goalkeeper, dribble towards Goal 'B' and finish up with a long shot at goal. During the whole exercise, a defending opponent tries to disturb play, but only with 50% effort.
- One after the other, the players run towards Goal 'A' and make a back-pass, which the goalkeeper has difficulty to get at. They then run into the free area and receive the ball back from the goalkeeper, dribble on towards Goal 'B' and try to outplay the goalkeeper there.

Game play

- A game is played with four attackers against three defenders and a normal goal mouth with a goalkeeper. The defenders try to keep hold of the ball for as long as possible by giving the goalkeeper back-passes. The attackers have to try to stop these passing movements and apply pressure on the defenders and the goalkeeper.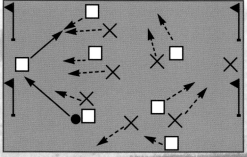
- In a game with 6:6 and a goalkeeper in each team on half of the pitch, an attack against the opponents can only be started after their own goalkeeper has received at least three back-passes. The opposing team can begin to try to tackle and disturb play while the back-passes are being made.

SENIORS

Exercise 9 TEAM TRAINING

Aims for the goalkeeper

⚽ Improvement of positional play in a game situation.
⚽ Catching flanking shots.
⚽ Defense against standard situations.

Aims for the attacker

⚽ Mounting a counterattack.
⚽ Improvement of team play.

Getting in the mood/Warming up

Work is done in groups of four including the goalkeeper.
⚽ The players pass the ball low amongst themselves.
⚽ The ball is played at sharp angles.
⚽ The pass is done with a ball at medium height.
⚽ A stretching exercise session is carried out.
⚽ The field players trot around with the ball at their feet and pass the ball high up to the goalkeeper, who is also trotting around with them. The goalkeeper catches the ball and rolls it back to the kicker.
⚽ This time the ball is passed to the goalkeeper low down on the move. The goalkeeper kicks the ball directly back to the player again.

Main training emphasis

Play is with the normal goal and two small goal mouths erected on the center line.

⚽ From the flank, crosses are sent into the penalty area. In the penalty area, four attackers play against two defenders and the goalkeeper, either to gain possession of the ball or send in a goal shot or a header. When the attackers are successful, the exercise is continued by another flanking shot being sent in. On the other hand, if the defenders or the goalkeeper gain

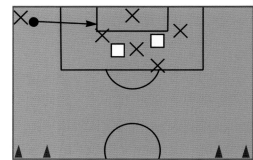

possession of the ball, they can immediately start a counterattack against either of the small goal mouths. The goalkeeper as well as a defender may do this together.

- To make the overview of the game more difficult for everyone, and to make players react to the situation, a flanking shot can be sent in from both the right and left wings.
- To make the accuracy of the flanking shots more difficult, a defender is positioned to disturb the delivery, but only half-heartedly.

Game play

A penalty shoot-out game is played at the same time as a normal game. Teams of 6:6 play on one half of the pitch, however, against small goal mouths without goalkeepers. The goalkeeper is in the other half of the pitch and waits there to carry out the penalty shoot-out. Kickers for this are those who have scored a goal already in the other game. He can choose a player from the other team against whom he will carry out the duel of the shoot-out. Which team wins the normal game and which team wins the shoot-out?

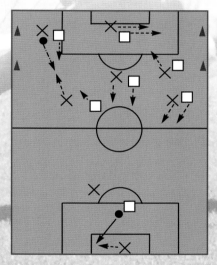

- In a game over the whole pitch with goalkeepers, the normal rules are used. However, for every free kick, the opponents may not build a wall. The free kick taker has, therefore, a completely free field of view to do his shot in, because the other players have to leave the path free. He has to kick the ball directly at goal.

SENIORS

Exercise 10 TEAM TRAINING

Aims for the goalkeeper

- Improvement of positional play.
- Fitness.

Aims for the field player

- Shots at goal from different positions.
- Fitness.

Getting in the mood/Warming up

The following exercises are done in pairs. The two goalkeepers can join up together for this as a duo. The goalkeeper, on the other hand, can be paired off with a field player.

- In pairs, the ball is thrown between each other in different ways. The distance between the two can be shortened down to four meters.
- The ball is thrown sideways to the partner, so that he either has to dive after it or take a step to reach it.
- Here, several stretching exercises are included in the exercise.
- The ball is played up as a high pass, so that the partner has to take a jump to get it.
- Several sprints after a ball, kicked by the trainer, are carried out in order to strengthen the sprinting ability.
- The pass is drop kicked to each other, but accurately.

Main training emphasis

The exercise is as follows: Player '1' kicks a flanking shot at goal from the right wing. The goalkeeper tries to catch the ball. The goalkeeper now sprints round the flagpole back into goal, while Player '2' tries to wrest the ball from him with his foot. Then, straight away, Player '3' kicks a flanker in from the left. The goalkeeper tries to catch the ball and afterwards

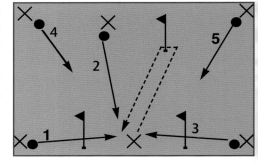

sprints round the flagpole again. Then Players '4' and '5' send in two long shots at goal. After this intensive work by the goalkeeper, he needs active recovery periods. This can be done by changing over goalkeepers or by taking time-out, during which the field players do an intensive work out with games on the move. The player positions should also be changed over often.

Game play

With the motto "Always on the move", the players must keep moving in the games which follow. The amount of strain, however, varies differently. It can range from a slow trot to a sprint.

- Play is against a small goal mouth without a goalkeeper, who plays with the remainder. The one team consists of three players and the other team, three plus a supplementary player. After each goal is scored, irrespective of which team scores, the supplementary player changes sides.
- In a game 5:3, both the goal mouths are of a different size. The goal mouth of the team of 5 is 5m-wide and there is no goalkeeper, i.e., the players defend it with their feet or bodies. The goal mouth for the team of 3 is only 1m-wide.

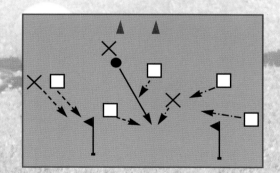

SENIORS

In goal – challenging for the ball in the air

17 FURTHER TRAINING IDEAS

In order to make training as interesting and as variable as possible, for the trainer here are further training opportunities, which he can use, according to age, to complement the previous programs.

1. In the middle of one half of the playing field, a 40m wide area is marked off. Play is 5:5 in this area. The goalkeepers stand on their respective sidelines and should receive passes from their own field players as often as possible. The goalkeeper gathers up the ball and kicks it back high up into the playing area. Each kick-off gains the team in possession of the ball one point.

⚽ Play again uses the same layout. However, this time each team of five can play with either of the goalkeepers and score points. The goalkeeper catches the ball in the hands and throws it out into play.

⚽ Using the same layout again, the goalkeeper collects the ball up with his foot and kicks it from a spot back into play.

⚽ Same game as before, this time the ball is taken on with the foot and directly kicked out again into play.

⚽ Same game as before, this time the goalkeeper plays the ball back to a field player who has just given him a back-pass. The team not in possession of the ball can only capture the ball while it is in free play on the field.

2. The players run around in the 16m area and kick the ball at each other to 'tag' them. The player, who has the ball, cannot be 'tagged'. The players have to try to make tagging difficult by using clever passes.

⚽ The same game can be played with the ball being thrown.

⚽ Using the form as in Paragraph '2.' above, a goalkeeper is now introduced into the game and he has to try and get the ball by catching it or diving after it.

3. All the players have a ball and juggle and dribble around with it. The goalkeeper trots around among them. When called out, the player called passes his ball to the goalkeeper who gathers it up and rolls it back again to the player while he is on the move.

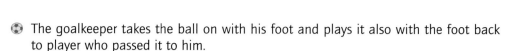

- The goalkeeper takes the ball on with his foot and plays it also with the foot back to player who passed it to him.
- The goalkeeper is passed the ball in a way that he has to jump up high to catch it.
- The ball is headed at the goalkeeper in a way that he has to take one or two quick strides if he is to catch the ball.

4. 10 balls are lined up on the 5m line, next to one another. The goalkeeper is standing on the goal line with his partner on the edge of the penalty box. The goalkeeper runs to the first ball and passes it to the partner and immediately rushes back onto his goal line. The partner tries to lob the ball over the goalkeeper's head as he rushes back. The same exercise is carried out with the remainder of the balls.

- The exercise can be made more difficult by lining up the balls 6m or even 7m in front of the goal thus increasing the gap for the goalkeeper.

5. In a game with six attackers against four defenders plus a goalkeeper, the attacking team plays against a proper goal mouth while the defending team plays against two mini goal mouths not protected by goalkeepers, but by field players who may not use their hands. For the defensive team, however, each attack must begin by the goalkeeper playing the ball. Therefore if the defender's team manage to get the ball, first of all they have to back-pass it to the goalkeeper so that he can start the attack.

6. In a marked-off area, all the players move about playing two balls. Both goalkeepers try to break up the play and get hold of the ball. If this is achieved the ball is thrown back into play.

- If a goalkeeper manages to gain hold of the ball, a change of roles takes place. The goalkeeper swaps over to become a field player and the person who passed the ball − vice versa.
- The goalkeepers play a competition against each other. Which goalkeeper can get hold of the most balls in a certain time (say 2 minutes)?

7. In a marked-off area, play is with 4:4 plus two neutral players against two goals with goalkeepers. The neutral players always play with the side in possession of the ball and serve to strengthen the attack. By using this majority, more goal mouth action is achieved and the goalkeepers are kept busier.

18 A TEST FOR THE GOALKEEPER

For a start it must be said that a test is very limited in assessing the various qualities of a goalkeeper. It also has to be adapted to the age group and ability level.

Defensive qualities

- The goalkeeper (GK) has to save five shots at goal from the edge of the penalty box.

- The GK has to take the ball off an attacker running at him in a one-on-one situation.

- The GK has to catch five flanking in-swingers from an opposing player.

- The GK punches away five corner kicks or deflects them over the dead ball goal line.

- The GK sets up a defensive wall for each of five shots and saves the goal.

Offensive and game play qualities

- The GK returns five back-passes directly to a player standing free.

- With a drop kick, the GK kicks a ball five times as accurately as possible to a player standing on the center line.

- The GK has to throw five balls to a player, as accurately as possible, so that he can take them on the run.

- After gathering up the ball, the GK has to kick five balls as far as possible in the direction of the opposing goal.

- With the ball at his feet, the GK has to play round an attacker. This exercise is also done five times.

Of course, it should be possible for any trainer to think up additional tasks to extend the tests for both defensive and offensive play. The tests become particularly interesting when several goalkeepers can compare their results.

Legend

Legend for the Exercise Games

1	**T**	Trainer
2	✕	Player
3	☐	Player
4	◉	Player
5	●	Ball
6	▮	Flag, goalmarker
7	·–·–·→	Dribbling
8	—→	Shooting
9	∿∿∿→	Juggling the ball
10	------→	Running (without the ball)
11	O	Tires
12	▲	Marker cones/poles
13	Ⓜ	Medicine ball

Photo & Illustration Credits

Graphics: Heinz-Willi Gerards
Photos: Klaus Bischops
Book Cover Design: Jens Vogelsang
Book Cover Photo: dpa picture-alliance, Germany

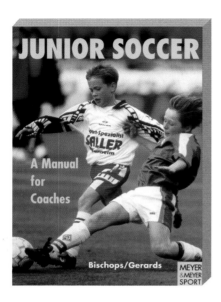

Bischops/Gerards
Junior Soccer
A Manual for Coaches

In this book soccer coaches and teachers will find around 100 complete training units for youth-work in clubs. Each unit contains a warm-up section, a section on the main emphasis in the training unit and a specific "winding-down" section with a game.

2nd **Edition**
168 pages
30 photos, 67 figures
Paperback, 5 3/4" x 8 1/4"
ISBN 1-84126-000-2
£ 12.95 UK/$ 17.95 US
$ 25.95 CDN/€ 16.90

Bischops/Gerads
Soccer Training for Girls

The focus points of this book are practice-oriented training units working around practicing and playing with the ball. Each unit – divided into warm-up, focus point and the implementation in the game – is laid out according to the players' age. Besides a purposeful increase of performance, fun is always a central objective.

160 pages, Two-color print
20 photos, 70 figures, 2 tables
Paperback, 5 3/4" x 8 1/4"
ISBN 1-84126-097-5
£ 12.95 UK/$ 17.95 US
$ 25.95 CDN/€ 16.90

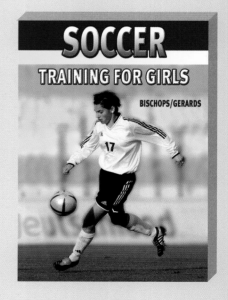

AnzGoalkeeper 10/05

MEYER & MEYER Sport | sales@m-m-sports.com | www.m-m-sports.com

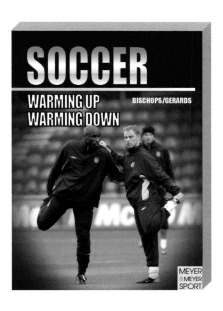

Bischops/Gerards
Soccer – Warming up and Warming down

In this book the authors provide some 35 programmes for proper warming-up and warming-down for soccer. The programmes are full of variety to avoid monotony and are based around the game of soccer itself, within a team situation.

2nd edition
136 pages, two-color print,
22 photos, 172 figures
Paperback, 5^{3}/4" x 8^{1}/4"
ISBN 1-84126-135-1
£ 8.95 UK/$ 14.95 US
$ 20.95 CDN/€ 14.90

Jozef Sneyers
Soccer Training – An Annual Programme

This book offers soccer trainers over a thousand ideas and methods for the whole training year with their soccer team. Soccer expert Jozef Sneyers takes you from the pre-season period through the season itself to the following resting period.

312 pages
Two-color print
More than 800 figures
Paperback, 5^{3}/4" x 8^{1}/4"
ISBN 1-84126-017-7
£ 14.95 UK/$ 19.95 US
$ 29.95 CDN/€ 18.90

AnzGoalkeeper 10/05

MEYER & MEYER Sport | sales@m-m-sports.com | www.m-m-sports.com

MEYER & MEYER SPORT